A MAN'S WORLD

A MAN'S

THE SHOCKING TRUTHS WOMEN NEED TO KNOW ABOUT THE MALE CODE

WORLD

MARK MILLION

NEW YORK

A MAN'S WORLD
THE SHOCKING TRUTHS WOMEN NEED TO KNOW ABOUT THE MALE CODE

ISBN 978-1-61448-164-5 paperback
ISBN 978-1-61448-165-2 eBook
Library of Congress Control Number: 2011943143

Morgan James Publishing
The Entrepreneurial Publisher
5 Penn Plaza, 23rd Floor
New York City, New York 10001
(212) 655-5470 office • (516) 908-4496 fax
www.MorganJamesPublishing.com

Cover Design by:
Rachel Lopez
www.r2cdesign.com

Interior Design by:
Bonnie Bushman
bonnie@caboodlegraphics.com

In an effort to support local communities, raise awareness and funds, Morgan James Publishing donates a percentage of all book sales for the life of each book to Habitat for Humanity Peninsula and Greater Williamsburg.

Habitat
for Humanity®
Peninsula and
Greater Williamsburg
Building Partner

Get involved today, visit
www.MorganJamesBuilds.com.

DEDICATED

To all the women of the world.

Past, present and future.

ACKNOWLEDGEMENTS

Special thanks to:

My creator.
My co-writer C.M.J. (Cupid)
for all your support and sacrifice.
Sterling Rain for your ideas, passion and spirit.

TABLE OF CONTENTS

INTRODUCTION

There is a secret world in which every man inherently belongs. It's an unseen world of persuasive male influence driven by greed, selfish desires, and dangerous dark motives fueled by incessant self-gratification.

"No woman is ever to know."

These thoughts and feelings aren't limited to your every day man but shared by the highly educated and powerful men of society as well. I witnessed this firsthand after having the opportunity to meet these high-powered men. From the biggest celebrities and sports stars to the wealthiest men on our planet, we all instinctively protect the male code because it gives us a supreme advantage over the women of our society.

Most women think they know everything there is to know about the men in their lives. The truth is everyman lives two lives. One is the deceptive illusion we are taught to present to society and the women in it. The second is the real man -only seen by other men.

Men discuss this subject openly in our social world but, never to reveal it to women because that would break the male code of silence. It's between men and men only... Until now.

Chapter 1

THE INITIATION

Claire tilted her head to the side, smiling while her three-year-old son Joshua clung to her pant leg. "You're going to be a lady-killer when you grow-up, aren't you.?" The sales lady cooed, trying to get the pouting three-year-old to crack a smile. Claire patted her son on the head. "Oh, it's alright, Joshua." She rattled on about one of her son's many escapades at a neighborhood playground they frequented.

Joshua rubbed his eyes with a half-balled fist. He knew what they were talking about because he gave a sheepish grin and hid his face in his mother's pant leg. "You're so cute." the saleslady said, grinning from ear to ear. What if Claire had a female child instead of a male? Would that child's behavior be acceptable like Joshua's or would she be told that she's far too young to kiss little boys? If little girls aren't supposed to behave like that, what's so funny or cute about Claire's son Joshua planting a wet kiss on one of the little girls at the neighborhood playground? What's so entertaining about him crawling under tables to feel some adult woman's leg? It's not funny.

Like Joshua, a young-man is programmed to believe his actions are cute and funny, but most important of all, he's being taught to believe

1

that it's just a game. In the case of a little girl, it would be shame on her mother if her daughter was kissing little boys. *What is she teaching that little girl at home, to be a little slut?* Don't you think Joshua will be too? This is just one example of how we program male children to become very demanding of women later in life.

Just two days ago Joshua wanted a couple of chocolate cookies before his dinner. His mother said no and refused his pleas until he started into one of his famous temper tantrums. This is how a young male child learns to ignore the word 'NO!' Some poor, unsuspecting woman just starting out in life will have to pay for his mother's mistake.

It all starts very early with men. A lot of the problems women have to deal with today involving men are caused partially because so many mothers are letting their male children get their way no matter what.

My father Travis Carr, was a very good high school football player, very tall, muscular and handsome, one of the more popular guys in high school. Girls would flock to him and my poor mother was no different, hanging on every word he spoke. Like so many schools with sports programs, the players were treated like Kings and the Cheerleader's were their trinkets.

This is an important point in a young man's life because we start to see the benefit's of being part of the male code. Their fathers and neighbors praise them and their schools love them, sometimes to the point of fixing their grades so they can continue to win those big games. It's no wonder so many boys want to become great sports stars. Obviously being able to throw a ball or catch one make's you far more important. Pretty hard not to develop a huge ego with everyone you know kissing your butt.

Men are taught at the earliest of ages to win no matter what… always push to achieve more and more. Our coaches tell us, "We won our last game, but we need to Win the next two." "Last year we won the State Championship, this year we must do it again." We must strive to be the best so we can belong to that elite winner's circle in life. Failure is simply not acceptable. This drive for perfection later finds its way into every facet of our lives as adult men. You own a very nice car, but you want a bigger, more expensive luxury car or maybe two vehicles. You have a wonderful house, but you want a summer home because winners have more than one zip code. You have a great wife but you can't see that because you're constantly looking for her upgrade.

Most women want a man who's successful and driven. They marry these good Providers, expecting them to eventually slow down and behave themselves after they're married. "I'm all the woman he will ever need," they tell their girlfriends. NO! he was a risk taker when you met him and always will be. Isn't that what attracted you to him in the first place? He won't hesitate to entertain the thought of somehow sneaking off with that attractive young woman who caught his eye because he's always playing the game and he just has to win that next prize. Remember, Coach said, "Go for it." Sports = Insensitivity = Ambition = Greed. We Men love games: hockey, football, baseball, even video games. We constantly strive for more prizes. Everything is a game to us, including our relationships with the women in our lives who are usually totally unaware they are part of it.

My grandmother Marilyn always took time out to tell Claire what a great wife she would be for Travis and what a great mother she would be for their children. She would never tell her lovesick daughter how she would be a great medical doctor or lawyer. She would tell my mother these things long before even meeting Travis, so when my naïve little lamb of a mother met Travis, it was a dream come true. She saw his charming smile and sharp looks and thought, *He's the one.* He was so tall and warrior-like. She thought what a great relationship they would have together.

When Travis met Claire, he must have noticed her long, unscarred legs and her firm breast, I'm sure he wondered how long it would take before he could get in to her pants.

Travis chose Claire not out of the desire for true, undying love, but to get laid and to do that he would have to prey on her weaknesses. Their relationship consisted of her constantly getting felt up, refusing sex, breaking up, then getting back together. After frequent break-ups and make-ups, I was finally conceived, according to Claire.

Claire was distraught. How could she tell her mother? Her family would think she was a disgrace, branding her as another blonde bimbo. Travis didn't have any obligations to her. *Screw her!* he thought without hesitation. *It's not my child.*

Claire was a virgin until she met Travis, so who else's child could I have been? She wanted him to be there for her and tell her that things would be okay, just like he always did when he wanted sex. He would profess his love for her and vow that they would be together forever because their relationship was special, not like all the other high school couples. It never happened. He never called or gave a damn.

My beautiful teenage mother dropped from being a sophisticated, straight A student to becoming a drop-out. Claire's family banished her from her home. All she could count on was food stamps and the constant terror of living In an improvised neighborhood. Desperation began to engulf her. This wasn't the future she'd planned. She wanted more for herself and most of all me.

By the time I was four she'd made amends with the family. Grandmother would watch me while my mother worked. Marilyn also babysat me while Claire got her G.E.D. Claire never stopped trying.

June was a hot month in more ways than one. My mother put on her tightest, cutest, strapless dress for a night on the town. I suppose that for women it's some kind of Summer tradition to see which one can out shine the other. That night Claire found a man's man-the type of man who knows how to get what he wants from a woman. Claire didn't know she was looking for love in all the wrong places.

Claire strolled into the bar with her three friends, all of them wearing patent leather boots. That year the Farah Fawcett look was in. That was the night I gained my future stepfather. He walked across the room with eyes ablaze for Claire, charming her with intellectual dreams. He seemed to have goals and the right attitude to capture them.

His buddies sat across the room admiring their colleagues maneuvers. For some reason, we like to see our buddies get shot down or revel in the glory of another male successfully getting a phone number. It's a wonderful spectator sport.

A year later, the sneaky, yet handsome, dark-haired gentleman she met that night was more than a steady boyfriend. Steve and Claire were now engaged. Claire pressured him with that age old question almost everyday, "When are we going to get married?" I think it wouldn't have been a problem had I not been there.

I remember at five years old how Steve would curse at me, practically calling me A "little bastard" whenever I did something he didn't like, but when he was in the presence of my mother, he was always concerned about my well-being. I was the other man in my mother's life and I would always come first. That was the big problem between Steve and me.

The situation came to a head one evening and Claire didn't choose Steve. It was a package deal. Steve had to marry her and gain a son. Steve must have taken too long to think about it because Claire packed up and we left only a day after that argument. It took about a week before Steve begged Claire to come back to him.

One day later, they eloped. Steve had gotten the milk for free and finally purchased the cow. My mother was a good woman, but what was the point of marriage? I wonder if it was vulnerability or the thought of her being with someone else that finally made Steve commit, or maybe it was really love.

After Steve married my mother, he tried to form a bond with me, but I felt that there was something missing-trust. I trusted my mother with my life because there was something special between us, but with Steve, I pegged it. I couldn't trust Steve as far as I could throw him. Later I would find out why I always felt that way.

Steve used to put me up to doing all sorts of things that at age five I never really understood, but I did them anyway. I can still remember the first incident to this very day. From time to time Steve and I went to the local park on weekends to play a little one-on-one basketball or toss around a baseball or football. On this particular afternoon we were playing catch. I mistakenly threw one just out of Steve's reach and it nearly hit a woman jogging by. Steve immediately had me run over and apologize to her. Steve soon walked up behind me, smiling and turning on the charm. I remember Steve and the woman fully engaged in conversation within minutes.

We went on many escapades like that. It's strange now looking back. At that age, I just thought my stepfather was a friendly guy. The truth was that Steve was a flirt and a cheat. It was right under my nose, but I didn't catch on. Was he just flirting or was there more? Steve and I both know the truth.

I couldn't understand why every morning in school my home teacher kept calling me a different name than my mother's. At roll call the teacher called me Joshua Carr, not Joshua Delgatio. That was my mother's last name. After all, shouldn't I have the same name? Almost every morning I had to correct my teacher.

On one frigid December Monday morning, I'd had enough. I sat in that tiny wooden desk near the window, twitching from the scratchy wool pants my mother made me wear, ready to set things straight once and for all.

"Joshua Carr," Mrs. Campbell yelled. "Joshua Carr, are you present?"

"It's Joshua Delgatio...Joshua Delagtio," I yelled. The class started to laugh aloud. Most of them loved my performances. Today, the audience was just as lively as the day I put a water balloon under Mrs. Campbell's seat cushion. Still, this was serious. I was getting tired of being called one name and writing down another. I wanted to be recognized for who I was, not for whom they said I was.

Claire hadn't heard about my classroom theatrics until she dropped me off at school the following morning. As soon as my mother pulled up to the drop off point at school, Mrs. Campbell came scurrying up to my mothers silver Cutlass Supreme. I felt a tremble in my stomach because I knew she was about to find out what I'd done. *Boy, I hate this woman.* I thought. I couldn't even get the car door open before she came running from the sidewalk to rat on me. Mrs. Campbell didn't lean her head into my side of the car window to tell of my foolishness, she went around the car to my mothers side. I knew I was in trouble because Claire gave me a side glance with the lowered brow which usually meant I was going to get it. I looked down at my dirty untied shoes, only to look up seconds later to see the two of them staring at me.

"Maybe it would be best if you spoke with him, he's so confused," said Mrs. Campbell, smiling.

They continued chatting as I was dismissed from the car. I'm very happy that conversation happened because it change my life.

Later that day when I got home from school my mother was waiting in the dining room to speak with me. "Joshua, I need to speak with you."

In those days many kids got spankings. It was somewhat rare for Claire to discipline me, but there were certainly times when I deserved it, like now. I was ready. I knew I could handle it. It would last three minutes at the most. By that time Claire would be out of breath, or start feeling bad for what she would be doing.

"Joshua I need to tell you something about your father." She paused. She spoke softly. The softness of her voice started to concern me. "Joshua this will come as a surprise to you, but Steve is not your father."

"Huh?" I said with a curious expression. I started to tear-up immediately. I didn't know what to think. As Claire consoled me, I began thinking about my real father, why didn't he come to visit me or write me. What made him abandon my mother and me? What does he look like? Amazingly enough at that age, I knew I'd never hear from my birth father. I had too much strength and pride to worry about some poor excuse for a man.

In the days ahead my attitude immediately began to change toward Steve. I couldn't help it, I saw him as just a family friend now. He was no longer special to me. I began to act out more and more toward Steve just to do it. I liked to use the Phrase, "you're not my father." At that age that was the only button I could push to drive Steve away. Every time I said those magic words, I was given new toys or clothes. Steve tried to win me over, but his bribes only worked for a couple of months and then I was back to my old shenanigans.

Eventually the joke was on me, the tables turned and Steve finally got tired of bribing me. Instead he got the go ahead from my mother to start disciplining me. If the bribes didn't work the spankings would. That was Steve's new mode of operation. Of course I still had my mothers heart in my hands and I knew it. I decided to tell her that Steve would spank me for little or no reason, whether I did something or not.

Her exact words to Steve were, "Don't you ever lay another hand on my son again or you will be living by yourself."

Later Steve and I would find a mutual respect for one another. We decided to just be friends since we both knew neither of us was going anywhere. Weeks after that incident Steve and I got much more comfortable with one another. According to him It was finally time to teach me how to be a man. To me it sounded like he was teaching me how manipulate women to get what I wanted from them. Steve explained that all men live under an unspoken brotherhood known as "The Male Code." He said that the code is very important to all men and that I would understand as I moved through life, but the basic rules were that we were never to expose each other's secrets and that we always cover for one another. Steve went on to say that all men have a way of speaking to one another without even saying a single word. This all sounded a little crazy at the first, but as time passed I would learn that the code was a very real thing.

I was about nine or ten years old and up to no good as usual. I wanted a little fun on a Sunday afternoon so I had Andrew, a school friend, climb the willow tree in our back yard and help me tie a rope to it from our clothes line so we could play Tarzan. Andrew swung first and let out a load Tarzan-type yell. I usually tried out my more dangerous ideas on him first and if he didn't get hurt then I knew it would be okay for me to try. I climbed up the tree and when I got to the tree limb near the rope I foolishly lunged for it. I was hoping to swing like Andrew, but instead I missed the swinging rope by inches and fell like a sack of bricks, knocking the air right out of me. All I could do was roll around on the ground grabbing my stomach hoping that god would grant me the ability to catch my breath. Before I knew it Andrew had dragged Steve out of the house rattling of the entire story, detail after detail. A pair of house slippers was all that I could see as I struggled to my feet. My eyes were still a bit blurry, because they were full of tears.

Steve didn't ask if I was okay, and didn't even check for broken bones, like mother would have done.

"Boy! What the hell is wrong with you? Are you crying? You're alright so quit crying like a little girl. That's for babies, are you a baby?" Steve yelled. My voice was still shaky, but I was able to squeeze out an answer.

"No!"

"That's right, your tough. You're a man. I don't want to see you crying like some little girl ever again. Understand?" He ran his hands through his hair and walked back into the house to catch-up on the football game he was watching.

I thought about what he said, and he was right, I was a man. I shouldn't go around crying at every little thing that happens to me. Every time I thought about it, my shoulders went back and my chest puffed out. So I learned another way to express myself when ever I got hurt, I would use what I call the "male-trum" The male temper tantrum.

If I got hurt on my bike, I wouldn't cry. I would kick, slam or curse at it. If my fingers got caught in a door, I would punch it. My mother started noticing a change in my behavior, especially when there were girls around. I was always trying different ways to impress them. I couldn't ride my bike pass a girl without doing wheelies. If I could showoff, I would. That's when my parents decided to sit me down and give me "The Talk." They gave me the "sex chat" all parents have to give sooner or later. Like most guys my age, I already knew just about all there was to know about the basics, but I let them chat away. At the end of the talk my parents made the statement which I'm sure is heard in just about every household in America.

"Don't even think about bringing and babies into this world while under my roof," my mother said just before leaving my room. Steve stuck around because had a little more to say.

"Now Josh, listen, I know you like girls and all, but if you find one that you really like let me know. I'll give you rubbers." I was getting a little embarrassed. The subject of sex is just so hard to discuss with your parents-at least that's how I felt at the time.

Steve wasn't finished. "I know when you have an itch you have to scratch it. Just make sure your mother doesn't find out. This is a conversation between two men okay? There's going to come a time when kissing wont be enough. I know what you and Lisa do next door that's why I'm talking to you like a man."

I started to turn red. He then got on the subject of wet dreams, and that they would stop once I had sex. Again he mentioned that he had plenty of rubbers when ever I needed them. Steve was almost demanding that I get laid. The entire time this conversation was happening, he never once said anything about the girl. It was all about me, and what I wanted.

In the eyes of my mother, I was too young to even think about having sex. In Steve's eyes, it was one of the best things a young man could experience. It would make me a man and it was time for me to have sex with the first girl who would let me. It seemed so very selfish now that I look back on it. Steve never once talked about having a relationship, only about using a girl for sex. Maybe that's why we men know how to get a woman, but few know how and what it takes to keep one.

After that talk with Steve, I felt I had the green light. I was already a little flirtatious, but now I was almost out of control. I would try and feel up any girl I could. Today, it's called sexual harassment. Girls were late on understanding boys at that time. We could argue they know almost nothing about us even today.

In my social studies class there was a girl that I could never keep my eyes off of- Sabrina. The teacher was big on forums, so she'd have us take our desks and make a circle so we could discuss topics with one another face to face. Sabrina's desk would always seem to be directly across from mine.

I guess her mother never had a chance to teach her that a lady always crosses her legs because Sabrina never did. It was a fantastic view for me. I always got my midday entertainment watching her panties ride up between her legs when ever she wore a skirt to school and Sabrina had a lot of skirts.

The things I thought about were so dirty. If it hadn't have been for Sabrina and her open legs, I probably wouldn't have half the imagination I have today. Just looking between her legs would make my pants balloon straight up. It seemed like every time I would be in my private little man's world, Mrs. Rhodes would call on me. She would ask me to give my opinion or worse, she'd have me get up and write something on the chalk board. I would usually begin a comedic debut to get my mind off of Sabrina's panties and back on class.

Unfortunately, I'd start the class laughing and giggling, which sometimes got me into hot water. Still, I'd much rather get in trouble for disrupting the class then to be called the class hard-on.

I bet you often wondered why certain male students would rather say 'I don't know' than to go to the board and try. Truth is, more than likely that boy has anerection he can bring down. If you were a guy, you wouldn't get out of your seat either.

Desperate times called for desperate measures. I was tired of only fantasizing about Sabrina. One day, both Sabrina and I were leaving our social studies class together. I made sure to follow behind her, getting closer than I had ever been to her. All of a sudden, I sort of reach around her and my hand ended up on her breast. I just had to touch a real breast. Sabrina just giggled and pushed my hand away.

To this day I can still remember that incident very clearly. I will never forget the way it felt in my hand. I was turned on instantly. Poor Sabrina just wasn't stern enough with me. I told everyone that she made out with me. I didn't go into detail because I didn't have any. The story I did make-up seemed to make them all believers and made me more popular.

Sabrina continued to become a victim of harassment from other boys. Things like getting her skirt lifted, getting her butt slapped, and of course the old boob squeeze happened more and more. All she did was laugh and say stop it. This only causes boys to continue because we begin to think it's a game.

Looking back I'm sorry I ever felt that poor girl up. It's strange how we men do things so very stupid that ends up hurting someone else, sometimes for a lifetime. I couldn't understand why she allowed us to do those things. Maybe it made her feel as if she was the center of attention or maybe she just hadn't learned how to use the word *NO*.

The following school year, I decided to move on to someone else. Like so many males, I soon got bored and set my sights on other adventures. I had my eye on someone new, Susan Massey. She was sort of the ugly duckling that at this time was fast becoming a swan. She was naturally cute with sort of a nerdish quality. Not very stylish, no make-up. She was just cute.

Susan was the kind of girl who always got *A's* on her tests and would be in the classroom minutes before the other students. One morning in our math class, I decided to back Susan into a corner of the room to feel-her-up. She looked pretty soft and meek, so I figured she wouldn't do anything. *Boy was I wrong!*

Once I had her backed up, I looked in her eyes and Said, "can I touch your boob?"

To my surprise, Susan didn't get scared or try to run, She just yelled "Shut-up!" as loud as she could right in my face. "You're the most disgusting boy I have ever seen."

I wasn't afraid of her, so I grabbed her breast anyway. The next thing I remember was getting a stinging slap in the mouth. Susan then ran to the teacher just out side the door. I sat down at my desk acting as if nothing had happened, although my lip was swelling up from the slap. *Wow, that girl can hit!*

The class started to come in and take their seats. I just sat there quiet. Trying to look innocent. We were only five minutes into class discussion when a familiar name was called over the intercom. "Joshua Carr to the principle's office. Joshua Carr, please report to the principle's office." Every student in class turned and looked directly at me.

I started that long slow walk to the principal's office, but I was in no hurry to get there. On the way I was trying to figure out what I could say to get myself out of this mess. All kinds of stories ran through my head. Somehow I had to make her sound like she was a liar, which would be hard. She was a top student.

When I walked into the office, I saw Susan in tears, telling her version of the story. She made it sound like I Had tried to kill her. I struggled to speak, only to be told to sit down and be quiet by principle Miller. After Susan was finished destroying me, she was told to wait outside.

The minute she closed the door behind her, I jumped into my role as the victim. "Mr. Miller, that's not what happened," I said, trying to look angry. "She's lying to you. Don't believe her."

"Now, now son," Mr. Miller said, laying his chubby hand on my shoulder. "I understand all to well what happened. You must understand that not all girls are like that Joshua. I know you're a pretty good student and I understand what your going through. I was a young man once upon a time myself, you know. You're growing up and becoming a man," he said, smiling. "In a few years you two will probably be girlfriend and boyfriend. Do me a favor and Just slow down, Joshua. There's no fire. She'll come around if you just give her some time. I don't think your parents need to know about this if you promise to behave yourself. Do we have an understanding?"

"Yes Sir." I said grinning. "

"Now go back to class, and for god's sake, stay out of trouble."

I left Mr. Miller's office feeling better than ever. *WOW! I think Steve was right.* I could do no wrong. Mr. Miller made me realize that there really was something to this code thing Steve talked about.

A fellow male would always do what he could to cover for another.

After that incident I decided enough with Susan. I thought I'd concentrate on my next door neighbor, Lisa. Lisa was much easier to get. After all she was just next door. She was always teasing me with sexual comments. Sometimes she would act as if she was going to let me see her breast, only to open her shirt to reveal another shirt on underneath it. She loved toying with me.

I always felt that teasing a guy was about the worst thing a girl could do. It's a shame that many men take teasing too seriously. I would just get over it and move on, later returning like a fool to try again.

Time passed on and I was tired of Lisa and her games, I was getting older and more and more aroused by her. I was getting sick of playing with myself in the shower every other day. I was ready to see and feel the real thing. All I had to do was sharpen my act with Lisa. I had only gotten to first base with her so far. My thirteenth birthday was fast approaching and I made a promise to myself to have sex before I was in my teens. I learned to be more patient with her. We would just study together and talk on the telephone. I started to understand that sometimes to get what you want from a women, you have to relax, become her friend but don't become too friendly.

My patience was beginning to pay off for me. I learned that Lisa's mother would soon be going out of town to visit family. Her father worked afternoons for an automotive company, so the timing was perfect for me to have a go at Lisa. For most young man, losing our virginity is probably the single biggest event of our lives.

Lisa's mother left early on Monday morning and wouldn't be returning until the following week. Lisa and I discussed having our rendezvous on Wednesday night. My mother worked early mornings, so she would go to bed at about six o'clock to be well rested. The only person who would be up during the night would be Steve, and he wanted nothing more than for me to lose my virginity.

Wednesday night was here at last. I was ready. I even sneaked a few spray's of Steve's best cologne to smell good. I got out my nicest cleanest clothes, and brushed my teeth twice. It was about eight o'clock when I flashed a flashlight beam at Lisa's bedroom window which nearly faced mine. After a few flashes, Lisa appeared. She opened her window and whispered, "What do you want?"

"*What do I want?* Did we or did we not plan this a few days ago?"

Like I said, Lisa was a huge tease. Tonight I wasn't going to be denied. I had been patient long enough. "Where's your dad?" I whispered.

"At work. Why?"

"I want to come over, that's why." I wasn't going to give up and she knew it. I hoped she was just playing hard to get and not getting cold feet.

Lisa opened her screen and before I knew it I was inside her bedroom, my heart pounding like a kick drum. It was really exciting. "So what is it you want, Josh?"

I looked her up and down in her over-sized baseball shirt. She had on light make-up and her hair looked freshly combed. She wanted the same thing I wanted. No girl gets that pretty simply to go to bed.

"Lisa, let's stop playing around." I said with a serious look. I was still trying to calm myself and be cool at the same time. I took her hand and sat next to her on her big brass bed. I knew what I had to do to get what I wanted. I hung my head and tried to look a little sad.

"What's wrong, Josh?" she finally asked.

I began my act. "Lisa, I've liked you for a very long time and you act like you don't want to be bothered with me."

"That's not true," she said. "I heard about you and Sabrina and I got a little mad. I kind of wanted you to be my first, but you'd already screwed around with Sabrina."

Boy did I screw-up. She'd wanted me all along or maybe she wanted me to think that because she was jealous that Sabrina had supposedly had sex with me. I knew I was going to get it. I'd always heard that a girl will want you more if they think you've been involved with their friend. They get curious and want to see what you're all about.

I pulled her closer to me and put my arm around her. I was nervous because I'd never been this close to a girl before. I pushed forward and gave Lisa a French kiss. As soon as I did that, she seemed ready for anything. It was obvious that she was just as aroused as I was. I pulled off her baseball shirt to get a look at her. She was beautiful in the moonlight that seemed to bath the room with a muted glow. I hurried to pull off my clothes, then sat back on the bed waiting for Lisa to take off her last piece of clothing.

She stood in front of me and began to pull off her panties. "Wow!" was the only thing in my head. I couldn't believe that I was sitting here looking at a naked girl. She jumped under the sheets with me following close behind. We immediately embraced each other. Her body felt soft and so alive. I must say, that was one of the greatest feelings I've ever experienced. It had to be no more than 60 seconds worth of sex, but it seemed much longer to me.

Soon after we were done, we both began to fall off to sleep, snuggled together. Later in my post climax daze Lisa was whispering and tapping me trying to wake me up. "I think my father's home."

"Oh sh**," I said. "I've got to get out of here!"

All of a sudden, Lisa and I turned and looked at each other with shock written all over our faces. We'd heard a woman's voice from the hallway.

"Sssshhhhh," Lisa said. "Be quiet."

I finished putting on my clothes while trying to listen to the conversation down the hall.

"Ooohh!" a women's voice said.

"Sssh, keep it quiet," I heard her father whisper.

The noises were coming from a woman, but it wasn't Lisa's mother. It sounded like they were in Lisa's parent's bedroom just a few steps down the hall from Lisa's room. Lisa's dad must have decided to have a little fun and games of his own. Lisa sat on the bed listening.

How could a man like Lisa's father decide to cheat? Her father always behaved like the perfect guy. He always seemed to take real good care of his family, as far as I knew. He was a quiet man who kept to himself. I had never ever heard him even raise his voice, not even once. For me it was hard to believe that he was no better than any other man. I guess both Lisa and I learned a lot that night. I kissed Lisa as passionately as I could and scampered back through the bedroom window.

Once I was back inside my house I quietly tiptoed to the bathroom. After gently closing the door behind me, I stood proud in front of the mirror and said to myself, "You did it! You're a man now, Joshua." I was so excited that I finally crossed over from being just a boy to becoming a full-fledged man, but my face hadn't changed yet. Rumor was that after a guy's first sexual experience you change. Your attitude was suppose to change as well as your physical appearance. For some reason I expected an instant transformation. *Oh sh**! I didn't wear a condom. Oh well, screw it. What's done is done.* I washed up and dove into bed with a huge smile on my face, thinking about the experience over and over again as I fell off to sleep.

· · · · ·

The school bell rang as I was running down the hallway just seconds before class was to begin. I slipped through the door and hurried to sit down at my desk while the teacher was busy writing on the chalkboard.

A classmate filled me in on the word of the day. Come to find out the word of the day was me. Lisa must have jumped on the phone late last night and told her friends that we were a couple and her friends must have spread the word. School had only begun ten minutes earlier, yet many students heard we were an item. I never told Lisa we were going to be a couple. Why the hell would I want that? She was just an experience, that was as far as it went for me. Lisa saw it a different way. All that week Lisa followed me around during and after school. Steve was watching everything we did. I guess it wasn't too hard to figure out.

A week later Steve asked me to help him clean out the garage, which in my opinion was already clean. I knew he wanted to give me the third degree. I didn't have two feet inside the garage when he gave me a slap to the back of my head.

"Didn't I tell you to get some rubbers from me first?" He said with one eye brow raised.

I said nothing, I just stood there rubbing the back of my head frowning at him. I was sentenced to rake up all the leaves in the yard for betraying him.

It had been three weeks after I'd had sex with Lisa, and now she was beginning to get on my nerves. "Where are you going?" became her favorite question. At school, she made sure to find out where I was and what I was doing. It's kind of funny how after you have sex with a girl they think you belong to them. Steve warned me this would happen. Not this man, I could care less about a commitment. As a matter of fact, she was blocking a lot of other action I could have taken advantage of.

My prayers were soon answered because it wasn't long before my parents informed me that we'd soon be moving to a new upper class type neighborhood. I wondered if I'd be able to score big there. Hopefully, I'd have the experience of some sophisticated girls. I'd heard that those classy girls cater to their boyfriends, buying them anything they want. *I bet I'll have those girls purring like kittens once I get a hold of them.*

The big day seemed to come almost overnight. The movers were down to just a couple dozen moving boxes left to be put on the truck. Lisa was waiting to wish me goodbye outside on the porch.

"I'm going to miss you," she said with a weepy expression.

"Lisa, don't worry. We'll stay in touch. Call me anytime you want. My cousin still lives near here, so I'm sure we'll get together." I gave her a kiss on the cheek and a big hug. As we drove away, I couldn't help but feel a little sad and heartsick. She was my first and I knew she'd always hold a special place in my heart.

Chapter 2

SCHOOL DAYS

I now lived in a neighborhood which was considered one of the finest neighborhoods in the state. It was very different. There were big beautiful homes lining the streets. Every Wednesday morning there were street-cleaning trucks that drove through the community. No one sat on their porches. All the lawns were well manicured and every home seemed to have an in-ground swimming pool.

There weren't many young boys my age. Many of the guys were four to five years older than me, so it wasn't so easy for me to adapt to my new environment. We'd been in our new home for more than two weeks and I still hadn't made any friends. I'd transferred schools in the middle of the school year, so many cliques were already made. I quickly figured out that if I wanted to belong I'd have to force my way in.

Girl hunting was slow and unsuccessful, even though I tried. Of course, being a pretty handsome young man, I did get some attention. A wink here and there let me know I had what it took. I did start too lose some of my street slang language, which was good. An upscale community does have some very positive effects on a young man. All these little rich girls didn't intimidate me at all. It took me a while to figure them out, but eventually I found out how to work them.

Over the next few years, I traveled back to the old neighborhood to visit my cousin. I also tried to keep up with the ladies there, but I never saw Lisa again. I considered myself a ladies man now, a sixteen year old Youngman. I didn't want any young ladies in either neighborhood to feel neglected, so I tried to spread myself around generously, flirting was fun to me.

There was a girl named Holly, who happened to live just across the street from my cousin Andrew's house. She was a hot little thing and I just had to have her. I could tell she wasn't a slut, but she wasn't a virgin either. I figured I could have some real fun with her. Holly had a part-time job at a movie theater so she was able to buy all the things a young lady needed to look good. I really didn't have a job except mowing lawns from time to time for a little cash and little old ladies didn't pay much.

Holly was a pretty golden brown color and at sixteen had a pair of breasts that just seemed to call my name. She was a short girl and that was another plus. I always wanted to try a short girl. The male rumor was the shorter the girl, the better the sex. Another rumor that many guys spread was that bowlegged girls were all sex machines and couldn't ever get enough. We guys will come up with all kind of weird and strange rumors just to give us a reason to try or do something foolish.

Holly was the product of a single-parent household. She was ripe for the picking in my eyes. I figured I'd polish up the charm so I could slip by any motherly radar. My cousin Andrew was seventeen. He'd been getting laid regularly ever since he was twelve. Andrew had much more experience. I'd only done Lisa and that was just a one time thing, doing one of the girls from my new neighborhood was a bit trickier. Those girl's mothers or fathers were always around the house. Still I had a plan to get around that-I'd find one with a car.

I mowed lawns during the week after I did my homework and when Friday came, I made sure all my chores were done. One evening we all sat down to have family dinner. Afterwards, I was dropped off at my Aunt Doris's house to spend the weekend with Andrew. My mother didn't seem to mind letting me go every other week.

My cousin Andrew was more like a good friend than a cousin. I admired him and he encouraged every sexual idea I had. There were many times while sitting on his front porch we would comment on different girls who walked by. If I said, "Man, I like those breast," Andrew would say, "What about that nice round a**?" He seemed to love taking my ideas and expanding on them. It was your typical man talk.

That's how most of our discussions went. We often talked about Holly and her older sister when ever they were home. We had some pretty serious plans for the both of them. Believe me this is normal for not just young men but for most if not all men. We constantly fantasize.

One Saturday, the games began. My watch was synchronized. I knew that Holly got off work at six o'clock and her mother would be gone. Her mother worked from four o'clock until midnight. Andrew and I proceeded up their walkway at seven o'clock. Lacy was sitting on a green and white lawn chair doing her nails. "Hi Josh," she said, looking up from her hands. She was a little bit curt with Andrew. Sucking on her teeth, she stared at Andrew and didn't waste words. "What the hell are you doing here, Andrew?" She sounded a little like a mob enforcer.

That didn't discourage Andrew at all. In one move, he was up the stairs to the porch and sitting just next to Lacy. "To see you, baby," he said, stroking her bare leg.

"Boy, get off of me," She said, jerking her leg away from Andrew. Lacy was a bit of a tough girl. I think Andrew liked that about her. She provided him with a challenge.

"Holly, can you please bring out some sodas?" Lacy yelled, Sending a drink order to holly from the front porch.

Seconds later Holly appeared at the screen door. She had a mousy little voice. "Can somebody help me?" She asked.

I was the first to offer assistance. After passing out glasses of soda we all gathered on the porch. When I sat down, I made sure Holly knew I wanted her company. I took her glass from her hand and motioned for her to sit down on the cement step beside me. She smiled and complied. I was trying to make the mood a bit more romantic by talking softly and moving slowly. Lacy's constant slams against Andrew didn't help me in any way, as a matter of fact their arguing was tainting the mood.

I couldn't contain myself and broke into laughter. Holly chuckled a little and Lacy even started to smile, seconds later over doing it and bursting into laughter with the intention of hurting Andrew's feelings. I could tell she got to him a little bit because he lost his cool. "bet you wont talk so much when it's just the two of us," he said angrily.

Lacy just rolled her eyes at him. Andrew gave a hundred-watt smile showing all his pearly whites.

I cleared my throat. "So Holly, why haven't we ever gotten together?" I said playing with the glass in between my hands. I took one hand and used it to rub her lower back. She was giving an answer, but I wasn't paying attention. I was too busy trying to look cool. I slowly leaned in towards her ear. She smelled so good. I thought it was a cool move because I'd seen a lot of movies where guys would do that. I figured it worked for them, so maybe it would work for me.

After about an hour of good conversation and horseplay we ended the night with a little kiss and a hug. I made sure to grab her ass a bit to let her know I'm interested in more than conversation. Holly moved my hands back up to her tiny waist. She didn't get upset. We just said goodnight and see you later.

Later that night, Andrew talked about Lacy and why she was so bitter towards him. Turns out he and Lacy had a thing going a summer ago.

He'd gotten her into bed but then decided her best friend would be a better catch. He tried to screw her best friend. Now their relationship had some kind of sick love-hate thing. I told him he could do whatever he wanted, but not to screw up my chances with Holly.

It was almost summer, the season that always seemed to get me super aroused with all those half-tops and sexy shorts the girls wore. I think the warm weather tends to make us guys a little girl crazy.

Chasing Holly every other Saturday and Sunday was becoming a chore. The most frustrating part about the situation was that I knew that she liked me and wanted it as bad as I did. I could tell because the more we were together the more she would loosen up. We went from light kissing and touching to complete making out, but then the hard NO would come. It would take all my strength to turn away at times and say forget it. I decided things were going to be different. I was going to get laid.

Sex wasn't the only thing that I wanted from Holly, I actually really enjoyed her company. We never argued and we had a lot in common. She was so damn good- looking I had to have her.

One Saturday evening we started things off the way we did so many times before. We walked a few blocks to a corner store holding hands, I kissed her on the cheek and hand to show her some affection. I'd spring for all her favorite corner store stuff. She'd pick out modeling magazines, chips and soda.

When we got back to her house Andrew had his head resting in Lacy's lap, watching television. They were all cuddled up in a blanket. They did this almost every Saturday night. This Saturday the girls were different. It was as if they had some private meeting earlier Andrew and I didn't know about. Lacy's smart mouth wasn't firing off at all. Instead of smart assed comments towards Andrew, she was smiling and almost enjoying his company. I had a feeling I'd get lucky this evening.

We ended up in Holly's bedroom. Her bed was so comfortable I would have dozed off if I hadn't had a mission to accomplish. I kicked my shoes off and laid across the bottom of her bed as she turned on her stereo system. She soon found a comfortable spot near the top of the bed. *So she wants to play hard to get. Okay.*

She opened a bag of chips and just kind of moved to the beat of the music. I touched her silky legs, making my way up to her thighs. She gently pushed my hand away. I decided to move up higher on the bed to look in her eyes. I then put my hand on the back of her soft neck. I pulled her towards me and gave her a long wet French kiss. I started pulling her neatly tucked blouse from her shirt but my actions were halted when I heard the word NO! That was the last straw. I was sick and tired of being led on only to be told no, so I let her have it.

"What the hell do you mean 'no'? You've been doing this shit to me for months. Fuck you and your games, Holly." I jumped up and slowly started putting on my shoes. I had to bide some time to give her a chance to try and stop me. I was busy trying to think of something to say that would get me back in after such a harsh out burst. I knew I had hurt her feelings because she just kind of lowered her head and bite on her nail. My head and heart was telling me I was wrong, but my sex-starved ego was telling me that I had her right where I wanted her and to go for the kill.

"So what's the deal? Do you want to be with me or what because I don't have time for bull****. We've been together for months and you keep playing kid's games."

I was as cold as ice but I said what I had to say.

"Maybe I don't know how," Holly whispered.

"What?" I said, sitting down beside her on the bed.

"You don't know how?"

I said the first thing that came to mind. "Well, you aren't a virgin, are you?" I hope she didn't notice the slight frown on my face.

"I tried it once," she said. "but I don't want you to stop liking me afterwards like my ex-boyfriend did."

It was time to turn on the charm. I touched her chin and turned her face towards mine. "Holly, I'm not like most guys. I like you for you, that's why I want to be closer to you. Sex would take our relationship to the next level. We're moving too slow is all." I buried my face in her silky hair and slowly kissed my way down her neck. I kicked off my shoes, not even hearing them hit the wood floor

All I could hear was Holly's heavy breathing. She was finally ready. She sort of nervously rubbed her hands all over my body. After a series of French kisses, we finally peeled off our clothes. I reached in my pants pocket and grabbed a condom. I put it on in record time. After a few more kisses and foreplay, I figured it was time. I was still a rookie since I'd only done it one other time, but I was sure she didn't notice a thing. I probably moved as though I knew what I was doing. After all, I'd played with myself quite a bit at home and that had to count for something. After we were done, it felt as though a huge weight had been lifted from my shoulders. It was strange but my head felt clearer and my body became very relaxed almost immediately.

After that day I made sure I visited Holly as much as possible. It was a wonderful feeling knowing that I could get laid almost any time I wanted. After a few weeks, family members started making comments about Holly and me. They talked about what a great couple we were and how we'd probably be married one day. Holly and I were pretty comfortable together. We had a very nice relationship and we were practically joined at the hip whenever we were together. I think it was because we didn't see each other all the time that made it so good. I liked Holly a lot, but there was no way she was going to be more than just a passing fancy. A guys got to keep his eyes open for better opportunities.

The end of summer was fast approaching. Soon it would be time to concentrate on school. This school year, I wanted to go places, which meant I needed a car. My goal was to get my own or find a girl with one. Back to school I went, probably destined for disaster because I was too damn horny to pay attention in class.

Sports came very easy for me. I excelled at football and basketball. I started to meet all kinds of new people-black guys, Asian guys, Spanish guys, even Albanian guys. Everyone at school seemed to come from a different place. The one thing we all had in common was girls. Every guy wanted to get laid. The was the bottom line.

I had a gym teacher who could make sense of anything. Mr. Dailey loved to discuss life and why things happen the way they do between men and women. There was one day I'll never forget. It was near the beginning of the school year and the topic was women and men. He said that women make the world go around. Of course I was the first to speak up. "Mr. Dailey, what do you mean women make the world go around? You sure it's not money that does?"

"Joshua, let me explain. Everything that you do in life has to do with women. You want the best paying job to get the best woman. You want a fancy car. Why? To impress a woman. You dress a certain way to be noticed by a woman. You may not be doing it now, but one day you will be." I thought Mr. Dailey was wrong, but now that I'm older, there was certainly a lot of truth to what he said.

There was another class I found rather interesting. It was an Astronomy class which at times, seemed to border on Astrology. The teacher, Mr. Puree, would wear clothing from the Seventies. Bell-bottom slacks and a butterfly collar shirt was his usual look. One thing was certain, he loved science. He was about forty years old and very thin. He'd usually start the class each day with the focus on stars and galaxies and end up talking about planet symbols and the meanings behind them.

Mars and Venus always stood out to me after he discussed them in class. He said that the planet Mars represented men and the god of war. "Sometimes this red planet can be destructive, cruel and selfish." he said.

He spoke about the planet Venus and how it is the only planet which spins counterclockwise, saying women have much of the same qualities as it represented love, beauty, and harmony. Mr. Puree often talked about the future of humanity and the possibility of life on distant planets.

To most of my classmates, I'm sure Mr. Puree seemed a bit strange, but to me he made a lot of sense. The universe is a huge mystery. I would just sit in class and sometimes stare out the window, wondering about the future and try to visualize the world thousands of years into the future. Sometimes I'd dream a little too much and end up missing nearly the entire lesson. Lucky for me I had Christian who sat at the desk right next to mine. He'd snap me out of my daydreams. It's always good to have a friend around to keep you out of trouble.

Christian was probably my closest friend in school. We talked about everything. We both had a class with Mr. Puree and algebra class with Mrs. Stevens, the sexiest teacher in the entire school. Christian and I loved to go to her class, not because we like the class but because we liked her. They don't have a word to describe how good she looked. I always seemed to get near failing grades in her class. It was all her fault. My last two grades were C's because I'd be busy trying to figure out what she had on under her clothes or what she wore to bed instead of concentrating on the assignment. She had perky breast that defied gravity. I don't think that I'll ever figure out how they sat up so high. Christian and I would just sit there smiling at every word Mrs. Stevens said while my mind ran wild with sexual fantasies. It wasn't just Christian and me who felt that way-the entire male faculty did. Every male teacher in school was trying to get at her.

Christian and I became good friends because of that class. He was sort of a wild kid. He'd wear clothes that were sort of torn and old looking. He loved to listen to heavy metal bands on his walkman at school and at home. We were two very different kinds of people, but we got along great. We'd go to lunch together and discuss homework and video games or we'd hang out at his home watching music videos and talk about Mrs. Stevens. Christian noticed that Mrs. Stevens would go to lunch and sometimes even leave school with Mr. Miller, the school orchestra teacher. Of course it was innocent, she just needed a ride home while her car was in and out of repair, at least that's what she told me when I asked if she and Mr. Miller were dating.

It was a surprise to Mrs. Stevens that a student would want to know something about her private life. The truth was I had money riding on her answer. Christian and I had a twenty dollar bet. He believed the she was doing Mr. Miller. We both knew she wouldn't give a straight answer but we had nothing better to do. I also started to notice Mr. Miller hanging around our algebra class more than the other male teachers, but for my own sanity I chose to believe Mrs. Stevens. I believed that she had a thing for me and she would ask me out one day. To me she would be the biggest catch of my life. She was stunning. Long straight black hair which fell to the middle of her back, a gorgeous golden brown tan that made her look like she walked of the pages of a swimsuit magazine and beautiful white teeth. She definitely could have made a run for Miss America.

I always pretended to need help in her class. She'd come strutting over with her hips swaying, bending over and asking in her smooth sexy voice, "what's your Trouble, honey?" She would put her warm hand on my back and I would stutter out my phony question. My goal was to get a good look at her breast, which at times looked like they were going to pop out of the top of her blouse. After she would help me I'd look back at Christian and smile. He'd usually snicker a little. Mrs. Stevens eventually caught on to my little game because she began to have a student aide come in to help her with questions from the class. Mrs. Kelly was all to happy to assist me. *Oh Well, it was fun while it lasted.*

I told Christian about Holly. He was happy that at least one of us was able to get laid. I tried to scope out girls for Christian, but he was a hard sell. He had a weird kind of look. If a girl was out for good looks she wouldn't be interested in Christian. He wasn't a bad looking guy at all, just sort of odd-looking. As luck would have it, Christian eventually did meet a nice girl, Someone who was a lot like him. The strange thing about Christian and his new found love was that they looked alike. They both had blue eyes, blonde hair, and they were exactly the same height.

Christian's girlfriend Cally was very unique. She had an interesting taste in clothing. She often coming to school wearing boots and black tights with lace gloves. I couldn't wrap my head around her strange style. One day during school lunch Cally explained how her best friend passed me every morning in the hallway and would like to meet me. I couldn't help but imagine what my mother would say when she saw some girl with purple high-lights and several piercing sitting in her house. She'd probably tell me not to bring any more drug addicts to the house again, and then she'd probably go into a "Don't use drugs" speech. Like most mothers, mine was a bit out of touch.

I tried every stall tactic in the book to get out of meeting Cally's friend Shelly until Christian mentioned that he heard from Cally that Shelly puts out, and I immediately changed my mind. That's music to a any man's ears. We met at my locker just outside of my first class. She was cuter than I expected. She had blonde hair, green eyes and a cute little smile. She was very California-like and tall, almost as tall as me and I was almost six feet tall.

I didn't get blown away by her. She was cute, but I went for more of the exotic type. Still, she was good enough to date because she put out. With Shelly, things were different. She was chasing after me. I didn't have to walk to school anymore because Shelly always picked me up. If I was short on cash, Shelly made sure to give me some. I suppose that was her way of saying she liked me.

Shelly was a nice girl, but there was something missing. Maybe it was her suffocating ways that annoyed me. Whenever we had conversation's, there would often be a long silence's. I hated that. I liked a girl who could keep a conversation going. She was constantly calling me at home, almost every night. The times she called would get later and later. My mother was becoming more and more irritated by the late night calls, which would last almost an hour at times. Our calls were usually nothing more than us holding the phone and breathing in to each others ears. You speak to someone everyday and eventually you run out of things to talk about.

After a few weeks, I decided to tell Shelly that things weren't going to work out between us. I practiced saying my, "We'd be friends," speech while looking in my bathroom mirror combing my hair. I decided to tell her the night after our movie date.

I thought about just how to break the news to Shelly all day during school. *"It's Over Shelly." No, too forward. "Shelly, I know we've just started going out." No, that's not it. Forget it, I'll worry about that when it's time.*

It was about six o'clock when Shelly pulled up in her black 4x4 jeep. I was dressed in my usual look, jeans and a black casual shirt.

"Hi babe," she said as I jumped into the drivers side and she slid to the passenger seat. Shelly often insisted that I drive her jeep when ever possible. She threw her arms around me and gave me her patented snuggle kiss. It was part kiss and part nose and cheek snuggle. It was cute, but it wasn't satisfying my sexual needs. Shelly and I hadn't had sex yet and that didn't help the situation. Maybe if we had we would have much more to talk about.

"Would you like a drink, Josh?" Shelly asked.

"A drink? What are you talking about?" I asked with surprise. "You know We're both too young to buy alcohol babe."

"Who said anything about buying it?" she said, smiling from ear to ear. Shelly reached behind the driver's seat and produced a bottle of rum with two paper cups. "You're full of surprises aren't you," I said, smiling. "Where did you get this? It's the good stuff."

"From my parents liquor cabinet. They have lot's of bottles to choose from." "Well all right then. We're going to have a good time tonight."

We arrived at the theater about twenty minutes early and park in a secluded part of the lot. I knew it was a strong possibility of sex, but I wasn't completely sure. I wanted to go through with it, but I knew if I did she'd never leave me alone. We decided to have a drink before the movie. I acted like it didn't bother me, but after my first sip my mouth felt like it was on fire. We sat there for minutes just drinking and giggling. I was still trying to figure out how to break the bad news to her. It was nice of her to bring me drinks and all, but I still wanted to get rid of her and her boring conversations. Fall was coming soon and I wanted to spend my Thanksgiving vacation with Holly. That was guaranteed sex.

The rum was beginning to take affect. My legs seemed to become warm and numb. I started to feel very relaxed. It was a very good feeling. Shelly started to loosen up too. I looked at her in a different way after drinking the rum. I was becoming aroused and ready to see what was under her clothes. She was sitting in the passenger seat with her legs open. She was wearing jeans so I just kind of stared at her zipper. I don't exactly know why I was staring, I just was. I suppose the rum had made me kind of silly.

"Are you ready to go in Shelly?" I asked, giggling slightly.

"No, Josh. Forget about the movie," She said in a slow, seductive tone. She cracked the window and lit a cigarette. *Oh boy. Here comes another boring conversation. I'd better put the brakes on this right away.*

After she finished her cigarette, I decided to say what I wanted to say. "Shelly, we're both so different . I mean I think you're a great person and..." I started to lose my train of thought. It had something to do with her unzipping my Jeans. Before I knew it she had her hand in my pant's.

"What were you saying?" she asked.

"Uh, whew. I forgot."

"I know, you were going to ask me to be your girlfriend."

I reached for the seat recliner and lowered my seat back as far as it would go and closed my eyes. I took a long, beep breath. Shelly was doing something that I'd only dreamed of. The favorite sexual act for men all over the world. *Wow!* This was an incredible feeling. I decided Shelly and I would get along great after all.

• • • • •

Thanksgiving vacation was approaching and my grades got better and better. I'd come straight home and do nothing but study because I knew if they stayed good, I'd be at Andrew's house for the entire winter break. I'd started bugging my mother long before she'd make a final decision. After proving myself, she said, "Sure have a good time."

It was the last day of school before Thanksgiving vacation. I was so excited about going over Aunt Doris's house I couldn't relax. I don't think I paid attention in any classes that day. That's how I got myself into trouble. There was a book report which I was suppose to completed over the break. Shelly dropped me home. I was in a rush to get out so she wouldn't be asking me a bunch of question's about what I planned for the winter break. I was in such a hurry to get out of her jeep that I left my book from class in it.

"Happy Thanksgiving, babe," I said before giving Shelly a kiss on the lips. "I'll call you later."

I ran into the house as fast as I could to change clothes because Andrew would be pulling up in his new Mustang any minute to take me to his house. My bags were ready to go. Then the telephone rang.

"Joshua, it's for you," my mother said loudly.

"Who is it?" I asked.

"It's Shelly."

"Tell her I'll call her back. Thanks mom."

My mother gave her the message. *Thank God Mom answered the phone.* I heard the unmistakable honking of Andrew's new car outside. I kissed my mother on the cheek. "I'll call you when I get to Aunt Doris's house, Mom," I said, closing the door.

"You be good, Joshua."

I walked out to Andrew's car all smiles. "Open the trunk, man."

"What's happening, Cousin?" Andrew said with a smile as I jumped in the passenger seat.

"Wow, This is some car," I said, adjusting my seat.

"Thanks, Josh. Let me show you what it can do." We sped off, engine roaring.

Shelly called back a little while later. She explained to my mother that I had a report due when school resumed after winter break and that I'd left the book I needed in her jeep. My mother told her I was visiting my cousin for the Thanksgiving break.

"Can I just drop it off for Josh at his cousin's house?" Shelly asked.

My mother didn't think about how that would create a huge problem for me if Shelly was to come by. She gave Shelly the address and directions.

• • • • •

It wasn't long before I was over Holly's house, locking lips on her mother's couch. I was so horny, I couldn't wait to get her naked.

"Josh, let's walk to the store." Holly said.

"Sure, babe." I would have probably done anything she wanted as long as I knew we'd have sex later. We put on our winter jackets and strolled up the street holding hands.

• • • • •

Thirty minutes later, Holly and I were chatting as we headed back down her street with a big bag of snacks from the store, when all of a sudden I saw something that almost startled the life out of me. Shelly's jeep was sitting on the curb, in front of aunt Doris's house with the engine running.

Oh sh**! I immediately released Holly's hand.

Holly noticed my shocked expression. "What's wrong? What's the matter with you?" she asked curiously.

Totally surprised, I was standing there, trying to think up the fastest lie I could, but nothing was coming which would have made sense. It had to be something believable.

Finally I had something. "See that black jeep right there? There's a girl that drives it who keep's following me. I think she's got some kind of crush on me. I've told her time and time again that I have a girlfriend, but she keeps on stalking me. She just wont take no for an answer."

The lie just rolled off from my lips. At the time I thought, *That wasn't half bad.*

Now that I look back on it, I could have been a bit more creative. Nevertheless, It lit a serious fire in Holly. She didn't say a word, she just fast-walked to her house and went inside. *I'm in deep sh***, I thought as I continued walking closer and closer to disaster. I ran my hands through my hair, trying to look cool as I walked up to the jeep because I knew Shelly had to have seen the two of us holding hands. Out of the corner of my eye, I saw Holly walking toward Shelly's jeep armed with a baseball bat.

Shelly was not intimidated at all because she flung her jeep door open and was in my face in no time. I noticed tears in her eyes. "What the hell is going on, Josh!" She screamed. "Are you cheating on me?"

Holly was close, so I went into my act.

"I never said I'd go out with you, I don't know why you keep following me around. They have places that you can go to get help for mental illness, you crazy Bit**."

Shelly's mouth just hung open. She couldn't believe what I'd said. To make matters worse, Holly started in on Shelly.

"This is my goddamn boyfriend, you better get in your little jeep and drive the f***away or I will kick your a** for you."

I had to take a double take to see if that was really my sweet, usually soft-spoken Holly. Her voice was totally different when she was angry. She was so Menacing that she even scared me.

"I've been with josh over a month now," Shelly yelled.

"You have any proof? I've been with him since the summer," Holly said.

"I sure do." Shelly reached in her jeep and grabbed my English book. She threw it at Holly's head. Dodging the English book, Holly dropped her bat and went for Shelly, grabbing her hair. I just stood there watching them go at each other, like most men, I loved to see a good cat fight. The whole sordid affair was quickly broken up by one of the neighbors. Holly's mother was home and had finally made it out to the porch to see what was going on. She told everyone to go home. Just a little beaten and bruised, Shelly got into her jeep and sped away.

I picked my book up off the sidewalk and headed into my aunt's house. My head was like a whirlpool, taking in everything that had just happened. I hoped that it wasn't over between Holly or Shelly and me. One seemed to have what I wanted and the other seemed to have what I needed.

In the end, I tried to keep both of them. I told them all kinds of ridiculous lies to keep them guessing. It's amazing to me how women will stick with a guy even after they find out he was cheating on them. They'd rather dismiss the facts and keep the man. Eventually I left them both. I got tired of Holly's constant questioning. She always thought I was cheating. With Shelly, I decided to break it off just to see what other adventures I could find.

It may seem unusual for me to have attempted a double life so early, but in our social world we all live a secret life of some kind. The double life is not frowned upon by our male social world, it's encouraged.

• • • • •

Time seemed to pass slowly. I was feeling pretty lonely because I was now a single guy. I spent Christmas and New Year's alone. I had to get back into the swing of things because now I was a senior and I had to get a date for the prom. After all, it was a guaranteed night of sex.

Luckily, Christian and I had become kind of popular, but the poor sap had become Cally's little pet. He was so sprung on her. But even though he acted like he was a teenage newlywed, he still tried to get a little secret sex from other girls around town. We did all the things that every American teenage male did. We got part-time jobs, went to parties, experimented with drugs and alcohol, and still came out okay.

Because of our blooming popularity I couldn't invite just anybody to the prom. That's why I had my eye on Angela LaRue. She was one of the most popular girls in school. Everyone liked her and respected her family, who bragged on their French Heritage. Angela always made it a point to talk about the LaRue family dinners. According to her they had all sorts of powerful people over for dinner, congressmen, senators, and many influential corporate movers and shakers.

Angela was a snob, but boy was she a looker, soft pale skin, hair like brown satin and beautiful brown eyes. She had awesome curves. She was pretty much in the same situation I was. She had recently broken up with one of the school's starting tackle's on the football team and found herself without a date to the prom. Angela didn't have any classes with me in school, but I'd see her almost everyday in the hallways. I had Christian give her my telephone number because they had U.S. history class together. I'd just gotten home when she called.

"Hello?"

"Hi, is Joshua home?"

"Yes, this is Josh, Who's calling?" I asked.

"This is Angela. Christian gave me your telephone number during fourth hour."

"Oh hi, Angela." I was a little surprise at how quickly she called. "Nice of you to call me. Angela, I've been keeping my eye on you ever since the beginning of the school year. I've wanted to ask you out many times, but rumor was that you were dating David Moss."

"No need to bring him up," she said. "Just hearing his name pisses me off. I'd rather talk about you, Joshua. I've had my eye on you for quite sometime too."

"You have, have you? Sounds to me like we need a get together."

"Sounds good. How about this weekend?" she asked.

"Excellent. Let me get a pen and paper to take down your phone number and I'll call you tomorrow to set something up."

• • • • •

Two days later, I had convinced Angela to come by the house and watch some movies with me. I couldn't keep my eyes off of her. She was a natural beauty. Her attitude wasn't nearly as bad as people had made it out to be. We sat around lounging on the sofa, casually talking about school. After about an hour I started calling her Angel. I decided to get to the real matter at hand, the prom. "This may seem way too fast, but Angela, would you like to go to the prom with me?"

She lit up like a light bulb. Her eyes seemed to smile at me with a look of relief, like she'd been waiting all afternoon for me to ask her. "Yes, Josh. I'd love to go to the prom with you."

I was just as relieved as she was. It was pretty obvious that we both were desperate for last minute dates, but we both tried to act as if we weren't. Angel started to ramble off all sorts of things we needed.

"What colors should we wear?" she asked. "I was thinking about a traditional black and white tuxedo for you, and I'll wear a long black prom dress."

"That sounds okay with me."

"We need a Stretch limousine and I want to go to an elegant dinner after the prom. Do you mind if I call home to give them the good news?" she asked.

"Go right ahead." *Dang, this girl is crazy, this is going to cost me a fortune.*

Angela was already spending all my money, expensive limousine, big dinner. The only thing I wanted to know was if I was going to get laid. She hadn't said one thing about a hotel room.

Angela was busy chatting on the telephone, making plans that seemed to be all about her. I had no idea that prom night was such a huge deal for girls. I think they just wanted to dress up in their pretty little gowns and pretend they were princesses or something. We guys see it a different way. It's was a night of guaranteed tit's and ass for us, a reward for finishing high school.

I sprang the news to Christian and Roger the following day during lunch. Roger was a friend of ours who often joined us for lunch.

"Christian, I'm going to the prom with Angellllaaa," I said, singing her name.

"Alright Josh!" Christian said, standing up for a moment to bow to me. "That's a pretty big fish you caught what kind of lure did you use to catch her?"

"Well, I haven't caught it yet, but I'll catch it after the prom, I'm sure."

"Have you made-out with her yet?" Christian asked.

"No, Not yet."

"We'll you better let her know what's going on before you spend money on her from what her ex told me, she doesn't put out."

"That's him. Believe me, she'll put out or she will be walking her fancy butt home." I said.

"Well," Christian said, "I know I'm guaranteed to get laid, how about you, Roger?"

"Oh yeah! My cat's in the bag, and boy do I have plans for her. I'm going to get my date so wasted she won't know what the hell is going on. I'll be taking care of her on our way to the prom and from it."

"Listen, Josh," Christian started, "Just get her drunk as hell like roger said. That's what all the college guy's do when they want to get laid. My brother knows guys who drop pills in girls drinks to make them pass out. Who knows with Angela. She may surprise you and be a closet freak with a drink in her system," Christen said, pushing his tongue inside the right side of his cheek at the same time moving his fist to his mouth simulating oral sex.

"Yeah, you might be right. I sure would like to know ahead of time. This prom shit is getting a little expensive."

"Oh, don't worry. After you wine and dine her, she'll be in the palm of your hand. Girls like that kind of stuff." Roger said, patting me on my back.

• • • • •

Guys will look for any angle we can get to get sex. It just wasn't in me to get my date so drunk that she would pass out to have sex with her. To me that always seemed like borderline date rape. Even today it's a plan men openly discuss amongst each other. To most men it's no big deal, but to me it always was.

• • • • •

The night of the prom I had everything planned. I had the limousine, the clothes, the corsage, the dinner reservations, and a little surprise for Angela, hotel reservations. Steve ordered the limousine for me in his name, as well as the hotel reservations. He had a friend who owned a limousine company so I was going to get one with a stocked bar. *Stupid bowtie,* I was trying to get it straight as I looked in my bathroom mirror. *This has to be the stupidest thing I've ever worn in my life..* I tried to reassure myself that things would go exactly as I'd planned. I'd get laid and have a great night. *My money won't be wasted,* I told myself. That's what bothered me most.

Money is a huge deal for us men. It's all about saving it and not spending it unless we have to. Our main goal is always to get what we can while spending as little as possible, especially when it comes to women. I could end up losing over seven hundred dollars with nothing to show for it. All of the money coming out of my savings, no thanks to my cheap-a** stepfather who never came up with money when it came to me. To make things worse, I had to meet Angela's father. I had successfully avoided meeting fathers all my life, but now I finally had no choice. Word was many father's liked to threaten you before you go anywhere with their daughters.

I looked in the mirror admiring myself. *You're one good looking guy, Josh. You're the man.*

The doorbell rang, and seconds later I could hear my mother talking to someone down stairs. It had to be the limousine driver. I rushed down stairs looking and smelling as good as ever. My mother started taking pictures as soon as I hit the foyer floor.

"Good night, mom. I'll be home in the morning."

"No, Josh. You'll be home as soon as possible. Don't get in any trouble tonight, understand?"

"Yes, mom," I said giving her a kiss on the cheek.

I posed in the living room for a few more pictures before heading to the limousine. The limousine had all the right alcoholic beverages. "Oh yes," I said out loud as I sank back in the leather seat. This is going to be a great night.

A short time later I arrived at Angela's home. I had never noticed that there were homes that big around town. Angela lived in a small mansion.

It had a fountain, lot's of windows and what looked like a smaller house attached to it. *This girl must be spoiled rotten.*

Her father must have seen the limousine pull-up because he opened the door almost immediately as I neared it, like he was waiting there. He was full of cheer and hospitality. Of course it was all bullsh**. Typical male acting designed to make you relax so you could be read. We men do this all the time. I was young but I knew the game.

"Hi, you must be Joshua," he said with a gleaming smile. "Come on in, son." Mr. LaRue was older then I thought he'd be. He was very tall, with lot's of wrinkles and gray hair. "Angela's still getting ready. You know how women are. Since we have a moment, Joshua, follow me to the study and we'll get to know each other a little bit," he said, smiling as I followed him to his study.

"So Joshua, what's your plans for tonight?" He asked, tapping his pipe tobacco in an ashtray on the table.

"Well, Mr. LaRue, we plan on going to go to the prom, of course. We'll meet and Greet, dance a little, have some punch, and when we have had enough, we'll close our night with a nice dinner. All in all it should be a great night.

"I see," Mr. LaRue said as he lit his pipe. "That's all your going to do?"

"Yep," I said smiling.

"Joshua, don't try and bullsh** a bullsh***er. We both know what the plan is." The real Mr. LaRue decided to show himself. I knew he would. His voice changed and everything. I decided to keep my façade up as he give me the stare-down.

"Mr. LaRue, I don't think I understand."

"You understand all too well,. You have a penis, don't you? Tell you what. let's make a deal."

"A deal?" I asked, still smiling, and trying not to laugh.

"You keep your hands to yourself and have Angela back in this house no later than two o'clock and you'll get to keep it."

Just then Angela's older brother entered the room and took a seat off to my left. He didn't say anything, just stared at me with a slight grimace.

"How does that sound to you?" Mr. LaRue's face was stone cold.

I wasn't going to be intimidated. I still planned on having the best sex of my life with Angela, even more now that he threatened me. I'll bet Mr. LaRue had sex all night on his prom yet he had the nerve to threaten me. What goes around comes around. My first thought was to tell him to go screw himself, but I wasn't in the mood for a battle so I decided to play along and tell him what he wanted to hear just to shut him up.

"Yes sir, I understand. I'll have Angela home before two o'clock, sir."

"Great, son. I see we understand one another."

"We certainly do." Boy was I full of it. Mr. LaRue took a couple of puffs of his pipe and was about to begin again when Angela and her mom strolled into the study, beaming with enthusiasm and excitement. Angela looked ravishing. She was wearing a beautiful black sequined prom dress. I felt proud she was my date. I was lost in a long stare until her father cleared his throat, hinting for me to stand up.

"You're breathtaking," I said, putting her corsage on her wrist. I gave her a hug and kiss on the cheek. It was a great feeling. Her mother had us pose all over the house for pictures. She was just as excited as Angela. We took our last pictures on their front lawn and finally got in the limousine.

As soon as we pulled away from the house, Angela poured herself a glass of Champagne. This was starting off better than I expected.

We arrived at the prom amidst a parade of limousines. We entered the hall as if we were already given the title's of prom King and Queen. The music was so loud, so loud that at times it was difficult to have a conversation. Angela and I greeted everyone we knew and even those we didn't know. Flashing colored lights and prom banners were everywhere. The floor was covered with confetti.

One of Angela's favorite love songs was played so we strolled onto the dance floor for the first time. Being so close to her caused a serious bulge in my pants. I was experiencing some serious lust for this girl. There was definitely some good chemistry between us. When we looked into each other's eyes, neither of us could look away.

We periodically sat down to chat with other couples as the night went on. Later we started to see more and more couples leaving. We both knew where they were headed. After another hour of pictures, dancing and chatting Angela was ready for dinner. We walked to the limousine with our arms around each other.

It felt like we'd been a couple for years. On our ride to the steakhouse and another glass of champagne, Angela started to open up. She told me how wonderful the night has been for her and how it was exactly as she dreamed it would be. To me she was a little girl trapped in a woman's body. She was so cute. I charmed her with my honesty and big plans for the future. I told her little things about myself, about my art work, writing, and how I had an idea's for a couple of inventions. I mentioned how I loved to stare at the moon on starry nights and how I enjoyed movies, even the sad ones. I had her full attention. She just listened, never taking her eyes off of my lips. I knew I was making progress.

The steakhouse was very dark and romantic. Glowing candle light on every cherry oak table. The décor reminded me of an old English library. We ordered appetizers, salads, and later placed orders for filet mignon and lobster tails. I had never dined so elegantly in my life. This was almost the perfect end to a wonderful evening.

While eating our dinners, Angela brought up the subject of sex, which surprised me. "So Josh, Have you ever done it?" she asked with an innocent look.

I was a bit taken aback by her directness, so it took me a moment to answer. "Wow that came out of nowhere, why do you ask?"

"Just a bit curious. I've never been close. I've talked with my girlfriends who have. You know, Girl talk and all, they say it's different for everyone the first time." This was turning better and better for me every second.

"Angela, I've got to tell you something. Don't get mad, but I have a room reservation at a hotel tonight. I thought that you might want to go there with me tonight. Let's just go there and let things happen."

Angela lowered her head and said nothing. I didn't know if she was considering the offer or was angry.

"Angela, Angela, are you all-right?"

She finally raised her head. She had a look of worry on her face, "Josh, I like you a lot. You've made this the most memorable night of my life. Believe me I would love to have sex with you, I just can't tonight"

"Angela," I said with a depressed tone. "Why not?"

"Josh, if I have sex with you and my father finds out he will disown me."

"What are you talking about? How would he even know we had sex?"

"Trust me, Joshua, he'll find out. He can almost feel things."

The poor girl was totally scared of her father. This is a perfect example of how men keep control over women. This girl was terrified of being disowned. It's strange to me that this word is still used today, Implying that your family owns you. Only pets and material things can be owned. This is something I'm sure millions of women have been threatened with throughout the world. It carries a lot of weight to a young lady who knows she will need her fathers money in the future to pay for college. It's a shame that a father would use this tactic to control his daughter, keeping her from doing what comes naturally to everybody. Fathers like this think they are doing the right thing but actually they are conditioning their daughters to fear the next man who enters their lives. It's a lose-lose situation. If there was one day in which you'd want to lose your virginity, I think it would be prom night. This is how the world of men works. They have to control everything and everyone, especially their wives and daughters.

"Angela, let's just give it a try. This is a great night. We could make it even better." I was trying my best to stay cool and press on.

"I'm sorry, Josh. I can't go through with it. Maybe some other time, but not tonight."

I was really pissed. I tried my best not to let her see that I was, but believe me I was. I felt used. She could have said, 'Sure, let's go give it a try,' but she was flat out refusing. I stood up from the table. "Time to go. Let's get you home."

The drive to her house seemed long and depressing. On the way there I sat quiet while Angela kept on apologizing to me. "I'll make this up to you, Josh, I promise." she said over and over.

We pulled into her long driveway only to notice that every light in the house was on. It was clear that Angela wasn't exaggerating about her controlling father. We stood outside of the limousine for a few minutes holding hands and talking.

"I meant what I said, Josh. I want us to be together."

We gave each other the deepest kiss you could imagine. We were both so full of lust. I grabbed her near the middle of her butt as hard as I could while my other hand squeezed her breast. I figured that would piss off her father, who I'm sure he was watching from somewhere in the house. I wouldn't be surprised if he was using binoculars.

"Angela, it's okay, I understand. Good night." I wasn't a good liar. I didn't understand it at all, but I decided to leave the door open just in case I could get another shot. After all, I'd invested almost seven hundred dollars in her and I wanted a chance at collecting later on.

I couldn't believe I didn't get laid on prom night. I'd have to go back to school and hear all the guys bragging about how they'd had incredible sex. Of course I'd lie and say I couldn't keep her off of me. After all, A man has to keep his reputation alive no matter what.

Chapter 3

TESTING, TESTING

W hen I graduated from high school I was not at the top of my class, but I did well. I was elated when my parents rewarded me with a brand new Acura sports sedan. I enrolled in a community college after high school to buy me time until I figured out exactly what I wanted to do in the future. Christian and many of my other buddies went on to state universities. They were all pretty good about inviting me to their college parties on weekends. I had three different colleges to choose from for parties. Almost every weekend there was something going on at each one. Christian's older brother, Brad was a member of a big fraternity at his college, so I was constantly invited to attend. The biggest difference I found with community college and my friend's universities were the women. The community college girls had little time for parties because they were focused on getting those grades up so they could get to a big school. University girls were far more willing to party.

I remember the first party I went to with Christian and brad. It was an off campus party not far from the school. It was awesome. It was heaven on earth for a young man. Alcohol, drugs and rocking music.

Brad was an upper classman with a lot of friends. Some guys brought dates, but most were fishing for those naïve fresh female coeds. The entire idea behind those parties was to get laid. The guys had it all set up so well. They just let the alcohol do all the work. The girls who attended were more than willing to get drunk. Once the girls had a couple of beers, shots were usually the next step. Tequila was the magic potion. I think peer pressure also played a role.

There were those conservative girls who would start out with just a beer, saying no to almost all the drunken male advances, but after an hour of her friends telling her to have fun and loosen up, she'd be doing shots and smoking pot. These parties were where innocence was lost every single weekend.

The guys would usually get the girls so drunk they wouldn't even know what was going on. That was the point of college parties, to get girls totally wasted in order for guys to have their way with them. Boy, did it happen a lot. Bathroom sex was the most common occurrence.

These parties also had a way of turning the somewhat respectable guys into rampant sexists. At times it would get pretty degrading, secretly videotaping drunk girls while they're having sex was the big thing. Doing "double teams" on a wasted girl was also a goal for some of these guys. I started to see I was a saint compared to most of these guys. I liked to play games from time to time, but to just humiliate or degrade women was crossing the line. No one deserves to be treated like a piece of trash. These guys got their kicks out defiling these girls and later laughing about It later.

I'm surprised that some of these girls didn't file charges against these guys. I guess the girls didn't tell because they probably weren't suppose to be there in the first place. They probably had their parents convinced that they just stayed in and studied on the weekends, but the lure of a college party was just too much temptation for many young coeds who sadly fell victim to the pressure to belong.

After going to these college parties, I soon realized why date rape is such a big problem on college campuses. These young wolves lead their sheep to slaughter every weekend and these drunken guys do not take 'no' for an answer.

Parents expect their daughters to go to college and get a good education in order to be something great in the world. Little do they know that their sweet little girls have terrible secrets that they'd love to forget.

· · · · ·

Before I knew it, I'd enjoyed almost three years of parties and dating. I was saving a nice amount of my money while living with my parents, but that plan was starting to wear thin with them. My parents were growing tired of my lackadaisical ways. Every time I turned around they told me to get a real job and start acting responsible. I decided to look for a full-time job to keep them off my back.

I pulled the curtains back from my bedroom window and something struck me. It wasn't the ice cold air that radiated from the glass. It was the realization that I was womanless, bored and tired of my parents. I had to get myself together. I got dressed in slacks and a dress shirt and hit the pavement. I was going to find a good job. I was focused. I called places that were looking for strong sales people. I knew I was a very charismatic person so sales was a good choice for me. I set appointments to visit three businesses that day. My second interview was at a high-end electronics store. This store was know for it's futuristic look and unique products. Word was that the sales people at this store made very good commission because of the pricey products they sold. They ran me through three interviews before they finally called me and told me I had the job. I passed the good news along to my mother. She'd already made me company C.E.O. even before I'd started. I told her to slow down. I had to prove myself as a salesman first before anything else.

I started the following Monday. It was a rough day for me. The existing sale staff treated me like I was a joke because of my age. The new guys always gets pissed on I was told. I decided to exercise patience. I learned what I had to learn, and then began to feel out the store. I got friendly with an older black gentleman named Earl. He was supposedly the stores best salesman. I was informed about his reputation immediately. My question was for a man who made almost two thousand dollars a week, why did he look as if he had just awakened from a long nap in his clothes?

The Earl, as they liked to call him, was a war veteran with a serious gambling problem. If I were making almost two thousand dollars a week I would look like a million dollars. This man drove an old beat up car and wore just two different suits every week. He treated me as if I was his personal assistant, but little did he know, I was quietly befriending some of his customers and making them mine. My fellow salesmen behaved like a bunch of crying babies when I started to slowly out sell them. They'd complain that I stole their customers and took lunch breaks far longer than I was suppose to take. Little did they know I'd gotten pretty friendly with Peter, the store manager. Peter was a six-foot-two Don Juan from Greece. He had eyebrows that connected and a funny hunchback walk. He wore the best clothes that money could buy. It amazed me that he had been through two divorces and still had money to blow.

When he hired me, he made it known that he wanted me not to take sh** from the other salesmen. He mentioned that my job was to prove that they weren't able to perform their duties as well as they did years ago. Basically, They had all become complacent. I was to break up the store cliques and do what it took to outsell them. Eventually some started to notice that Peter had my back, they slowly began to give me some respect. After the first six months they knew I wasn't kidding around. I made top three in sales four out of the six months. I was becoming the top dog and I liked it. Peter pulled earl and me aside one night before closing and asked if we were up to going out and talking shop. I checked my wallet to make sure I had my fake I.D. on me. I knew that when grown men went out, it meant a bar.

We all met at a little dive bar downtown. This place was in need of some serious renovation. It was a little bar which at first glance you would think it was abandoned. The chairs had holes and looked like they were twenty years old. The tables were little, some written and carved on. It was very smoky and dimly lit. I was very nervous. Earl and Peter weren't nervous at all. The neighborhood wasn't the best so I kept wondering if my precious Acura was going to be ok. There were maybe twelve people inside. I whispered to Earl, asking why Peter would bring us to such a low class place.

"Because man," Earl started. "A place like this is where the easy trim is and you don't have to worry about running into anyone you know. Plus, we wanted to make sure you would be able to drink. They wont check your I.D. here."

"Oh, That makes since." I said.

The cocktail waitress was wearing her street clothes and was definitely lacking in the manners department. She didn't ask if she could help us, She just stood there looking at us until we noticed her. We placed our drink orders and patiently waited for her return. It didn't take long for Peter to show his true colors. After our first round, we all started to open up.

Peter was like a jackal. All he talked about was how he wanted to terminate people to replace them with a better sales staff. He and Earl chatted away while I continued checking out the bar and the people in it. I was sipping on my run and coke just listening.

"Earl," Peter said, leaning closer to Earl. "You remember what my wife looks like don't you?"

"Which one?" Earl asked with a chuckle.

"Lorraine."

"Yeah, what about her?" Earl asked.

"Doesn't that kind of look like her sitting over there?" Peter pointed to a woman sitting at the bar with her back towards us.

"I don't have my glasses with me, Pete. I think I left them in the car." Earl squinted trying to see. "Hell no, Pete. That's not her. Your just paranoid."

"You know how it is," Peter said. "After a few drinks they all start to look the same. By the way, have you seen that sweet little piece that comes in to see me at work? The one with the big breast."

Earl scratched his ear, perplexed. He was trying to remember.

"Come on, Earl, you know the one. She drives the black Honda."

"Oh, oh yeah, I remember," Earl said.

"Well, when you see her in the store tomorrow, point her out to Josh for me. My wife has been popping in unannounced lately and with my luck, they'll probably come in at the exact same time. I may need one of you guys to intercept. The last thing I need is for Lorraine to screw up my chances with her.

Earl gave a half laugh, half cough. I nodded, agreeing to go along with the plan. Peter must have had a crystal ball because the following day his wife and his girlfriend both were sighted. Peter had seen them both come in, so he disappeared. We covered for him, telling them both that Peter must have stepped out for a meeting. His wife immediately left but his girlfriend hung around, probably making a shopping list of things for Peter to buy her. What a weak man Peter was hiding from his own wife. I guess he was afraid of getting another divorce, seeing that he was always up to something. It was almost like a game to him. He enjoyed it.

One day I asked him why he got married again after two failed marriages. "Josh, I get more action married than single," he said. "Women like to cheat with married men. It's challenging to them. I also like having a wife to take care of the home. It's the best of both worlds."

Peter was totally controlled by his penis, like the great majority of us men. He was so promiscuous that he would secretly get tested for S.T.D'S on a regular basis. He couldn't get enough sex. I think it was his was of proving to himself that he still had it. There were times when I thought Peter was just lying when he'd brag about his sexual escapades, but as I got to know him better I became a believer.

One night in June we had a "midnight madness" event. Being open until midnight turned out to be too much for Peter. I wanted to get out as soon as possible, because I had plans for a late night rendezvous with a new female acquaintance of mine. I was in such a rush I had forgotten my suit jacket. Realizing that I didn't have it as I was opening my car door, I hurried back in to the store to get it. While looking for it in the office, I noticed that Peter and Audrey were no where around. Audrey was one of our part-time sales associates. It wasn't long before I heard the sounds of clothes rustling and lips smacking coming from the stock room next to the office. I would have never guessed that Peter and Audrey were involved. The kind of women Peter usually were attracted to were pretty stylish. He liked them very pretty and thin. Audrey was nothing like that. I always assumed she was a lesbian. Audrey was the only women I knew that was taller than most men, and wore men's dress shirts. She wore very little make-up and almost never wore high heels. I guess when Peter has to have it, he's going to get it. I decided to just leave and let them have their fun, I'd just pick up the jacket when I report to work tomorrow.

I drove home laughing to myself about what had just happened. I started to think about all the characters I worked with for eight to ten hours a day. *That Earl is something else.* This guy was two sandwiches shy of a picnic. He simply hated women. I think he had issues with women because they didn't find him attractive. He was a total misogynist. Earl treated women as though they were beneath him. He often said women were only good for one thing. I can't count the number of times I've heard men say this in my life. Get four of five guys together hanging out on any night and it's a given that at least one of them say it. Earl had never been married and his idea world was one where he could have sex with any woman he wanted and the ones he didn't he'd have hooking to make him money. Earl had some serious screws loose.

Earl did have a girlfriend named Monique. She was somewhere in her late thirties, but looked like as if she was in her mid forties. Earl would often tell us stories about their relationship. He especially liked repeating the story about the day he knocked two of her teeth out. In his words, he said. "She talked to damn much." I couldn't understand why Monique stayed with him for over six years being beat up, cheated on, and simply treated like trash. She seemed like a sweet person when she'd come to the store to meet him for lunch. She was polite and always smiled. With a life like that I wonder what she had to smile about.

• • • • •

For the next several months, I was really starting to get my life together. I started saving money . I spent my days working and my nights clubbing and dating. I was having a good run. One day, it all came to a screeching halt.

Her name was Amy and from the moment we met I couldn't stop thinking about her. The way she walked, talked, and smiled got my attention. When I first saw her enter the store, I immediately rushed over to see if she needed assistance. "Hi, Need any help today, Miss?" I asked.

"Hi, I'm thinking about hosting a little get together for Christmas and was looking for a new system with a multiple disk changer." I was staring as she spoke, so I used it as my opener.

"Sorry, I didn't mean to stare, but has anyone ever told you just how stunning you are?" I was full of it, but I knew that compliments are always a great ice breaker.

She cracked a smile. "No, I can't say that anyone has, not the way you said it." "My name is Josh. let me show you what we have." I would lead her to each item and stood back and watch her while I talked about the features. She had a cute little butt and my mind started to go into man fantasy mode. I envisioned myself taking off her blouse and slowly kissing her down the center of her back in my mind. Our male minds do this anytime we find a woman we think is attractive. We soon found the perfect disk player and we were off to the cashier. I gave her my business card and asked her to come back and see me. I was tempted to ask for her number but didn't. I had a feeling she'd be back. My eyes were still glued to her butt, as she waved goodbye and left.

"Did you get the number?" said voice said from behind me. I knew who it was.

"No, Luke, she got mine," I said, lying with a straight face.

"Yeah, right. You missed out on that. You probably couldn't have handled it anyway young buck," Luke said, grabbing his crotch. "If It was me I'd be over her house tonight giving her the Luke bed press.

I laughed. "You'd be playing with yourself, just as you do every night, Luke."

Luke was a big time fitness nut, Part-time salesman, part-time body builder. He was as wide as a doorway and almost all muscle. We all assumed he was on steroids because none of us guys ever saw him take a piss at the urinals. He always went into the stalls. In our male world, if a guy is never seen pissing next to other men, he's hiding something big. We figured he was probably shooting himself up with steroids when he was in there. He had far more energy than your average man. Most guys know how to use charm and tact to get what we want from woman. Luke didn't seem to have either. He wasn't a bad-looking guy, I suppose. I think his body did most of the work for him. The lady's loved his body, but the minute he started to speak he'd usually scare them off. He'd say some of the absolute worst things to women. Anything that came to mind.

When a guys trying to get laid, the last thing you want to say to a woman are the things that pop into our heads. If all men of the world said what we thought, none of us would ever get laid and most of us would be arrested. The smart men say very little and let women do all the talking. We just play along like were interested, even though we usually aren't.

Obviously Luke never learned this lesson or simple didn't care. In his opinion gyms were whorehouses created for men to get laid without spending a lot of money. He liked to play the personal trainer game on them. It's a common strategy we men use. He had his little business cards made up and everything. Anytime there was a young lady that came in browsing, Luke would try his best to out run me to help them, then immediately go into his personal trainer routine telling them how he could help them workout in a way that would benefit them. Of course, it was all a game to get them into bed and get the women to pay him to do it. These personal trainers types think they're genius. He loved to use test jokes on women. Most of us men do this to try and figure a woman out, depending on how she responds to our sometimes strange or crass jokes tells us exactly how much we can get away with. If a women was ever shocked or taken aback by what we said, we just cover it by saying, "I was just kidding" or "It was just a joke." We men have all kinds of tricks.

One Saturday evening at work, Luke went on about one of his one-night stands with some woman that he use to train at the gym. He often got carried away when ever he told a story. This night was no exception. The store had women and a couple children in it but Luke didn't care. He told one of his usual crass, sexist stories as loud as he could. Luke had some serious screws loose.

The great majority of men I've met are naturally dogmatic but guys like Luke take it to an entirely new level. Luke and men like him live to dominate women. It's an ego thing. Men like this are the worst men for women to run into, men who have a really dark almost sadistic side to them.

Later that night, I worked harder than usual and felt every bit of it in my feet. I was so tired my shoulders felt like wet sand bags. The drive home was a mess, traffic bumper to bumper because of an accident. *Oh sh**!* I still have to go Christmas shopping! How did Saturday get here so fast? It was only a few days before Christmas and I hadn't picked up one gift. I quickly changed lanes and minutes later turned into the mall parking lot. It was filled with the cars of Christmas shoppers.

I entered the mall, quickly scanning every dress rack for some kind of gift for my mother as if I knew what size she wore. I needed to slow down and think about a gift that would work. Something told me to go to the cosmetic department. I couldn't go wrong with a nice bottle of perfume as a gift. I walked quickly through the ladies fashion's department, dodging strollers. Later, making a right turn into the cosmetic's department. I heard a voice coming from my left as I looked though the perfume cases. "Need some help

"Hey," I said, turning to see a familiar face. "I know you."

"Oh my God! Your the guy who helped me at the electronics store," she said, smiling.

"Josh," I said, gently reminding her what my name is.

"Amy," she said, extending her hand for a hand shake.

"Nice to met you again, this has got to mean something, Amy," I said, smiling. "No way this is just some kind of coincidence."

"Maybe it cosmic," she said, moving her hands and fingers slowly from left to right. Like a magician.

"What are you doing here?" I asked. "Do you work here?"

"Oh no, I'm not actually employed buy the store. I'm a cosmetic representative. During Christmas and other holidays, my company sends me into stores to fill and supply cosmetic lines and introduce new products," she said, running her hands through her raven black hair.

We continued to chat for minutes, getting to know each other a little. She suggested a new perfume for my mother which had just been released to stores. I bought the perfume and got a free gift bag with it. I headed home with a great gift for my mother and Amy's telephone number.

• • • • •

New Year's Eve would be our first date. We had plans to start out the night with a bite to eat before the New Year's celebration. I learned that Amy was twenty seven years old. I had never dated anyone over twenty two years old. She wasn't shy at all and was willing to try new things. We went to one of my favorite restaurants where I introduced her to one of my favorite dishes, Squid salad. After dinner she took me to her favorite club for New Year's Eve.

I didn't even have to show my fake I.D. as we entered because Amy was known there. She had a booth reserved for us. This club was pretty unique. Pastel colored walls with all kinds of abstract works of art lined the walls. Most outlined with neon lights. The booth's table top was a shiny black Lacquer.

Amy was very attentive to me, making sure that I was enjoying myself. It was a new experience having a woman almost seven years older than me. Landing an older woman is a conquest for a Young man. This women had a lot of style as well as a great figure. I just loved the way she was dressed. She wore a pink satin cocktail dress that fit her cute little body like a glove, long crystal earrings and pink high heel shoes.

The countdown for the New Year had officially started and instead of joining everyone on the dance floor, Amy and I sat in our booth, finishing off our champagne, Ready to lock lips the minute the clock struck twelve. I heard "Happy New Year!" cheers as we kissed. Later, after more dancing, drinking and kissing. I asked Amy to drive because the champagne had really did a number on me. I was in no condition to drive.

Nature's alarm clock glared into my face, waking me from my sleep. I heard Amy's sweet voice. "Ah, you're awake." Opening my eyes and seeing her beautiful smile brought a warmth to my heart. I wasn't hung over to the point of nausea, but I did have a little headache. Suddenly I realized I was in her home, laying on her couch. Amy gave me aspirin and coffee, then turned on some easy listening music. I took a good look around her place. She was doing very well for herself. The condo was huge and fully furnished. I really liked this woman. I decided I should let her know that I still live at home with my parents. I didn't want any secrets between us. She didn't mind and said she figured that I did. She was so cool about everything, it was shocking. Something had to be wrong with her. I'd bet anything that she was some sort of closet sadomasochist or something.

As I sat on the couch watching her clean-up, I noticed I awoke with a strawberry shortcake blanket on me. I decided to ask her about it.

"Oh, some of my friends have children and sometimes they leave stuff here when I baby sit for them," she said.

"Oh, ok." I said. I also decided to ask her about a picture I noticed on her end table of her and two small children. She said she took that picture at a park while visiting with a few friends and their children.

"I love children," she said. "Why the interrogation?"

"No interrogation, babe. I'm just not into kids. to be honest, they bother me," I said with a little chuckle. *Great, she's child free, I'm child free. This could be a lot of fun.*

Amy had it together. She had maturity, her own condo, a new car, and seemed to enjoy her job. She was constantly traveling. Part of her job was to train other representatives in other states as well as keeping up-to-date on the latest products in the cosmetics world.

• • • • •

My mother and stepfather continued to ride me. It seemed that as soon as I had proved I could hold a job, it was time for me to go. Having a girlfriend in her late twenties also added fuel to the fire. I kind of enjoyed the free meals and housing. I kept my room spotless for them. Actually, I had little choice because I'd get a daily reminder. I started paying a few hundred dollars a month to keep them off my Back, but soon that wasn't enough. The push was on for me to leave. In the beginning, there would always be leftover's in the kitchen waiting for me with a note of some kind telling me what to eat after I got off work. Those days were over.

There was no more note and definitely no food. Instead of eating and going to bed, I had to leave out in the middle of the night to search for something to eat. I never really knew what I wanted, so it would sometimes take up to an hour before I'd find something I was in the mood for. I'd fall asleep late, unless they turned up the heat to ninety degrees to make me uncomfortable and toss and turn all night. If it was a Sunday a grocery list would sometimes be left for me to take care of. They were pulling out all the stops. That's why when my days off came, I was nowhere to be found.

• • • • •

"Thank God I'm legal," I whispered as I cut my fake I.D. into pieces. My parents were out working and the house was nice and quiet, so quiet that my mind began to wonder. I mentally went back to the first club I got into using it. *I can't believe they let me in with this thing,*. I thought as I sweep the pieces into the trash can. I was so out of place.

Off I went to the Department of Motor Vehicles to get my license renewed. I must have stood in that line for an hour. I kept myself busy by checking out the two hot girls that were a few spots ahead of me. They had on short little jacket's with tight jeans and high heel boots. I love to see women in tight pants, especially when they have a nice body to fill them. These two knew they were drawing attention and they loved it.

I started to think about Amy, and how I really liked her and even thought about what it would be like moving in with her, so I couldn't fuck up. Not just yet. I had to keep my perfect gentleman disguise up as long as possible. She was in Chicago on business and we would celebrate my birthday together when she got back. I felt like a little boy. I just couldn't wait to see her. I finally wrestled my way out of the D.M.V. It took a while, but that wasn't going to ruin my day. I was gong to have a great twenty-first birthday no matter what. Later in the day I got a call from work at about six o'clock asking me to come in for a couple hours because a salesman had a family emergency and had to go. I was a little pissed at first but thought, *Okay, It's for the boys…they need me.*

I walked into the store about forty minutes later, I noticed Earl, Luke, and Peter all putting on their coats like they were leaving. "You've got to be kidding me. Where in the hell are you guys going?" I asked.

"Peter started to laugh."

"To your birthday party." Earl said, smiling.

"You didn't think we'd forget your twenty-first birthday, did you?" Luke said.

"This is your day, youngster. Tony and Jim are going to lock up tonight because we have a little something planned for you." Peter said.

I couldn't believe it. We argue almost everyday with one another, we accuse each other of wrongdoing and yet they thought enough of me to surprise me. I started to realize that male camaraderie trumps everything in the end. It was just like Steve told me long ago, men stick together no matter what. That's what the code is all about.

"We are going to take you to the best Topless bar in town," Peter said, grinning.

We all jumped in our car's and followed Peter. Before long we found ourselves valet parking in front of the cities best strip club. My birthday landed on the right night because the sign out front said "Amateur night contest." This was my very first time inside of a real topless bar. I had been to countless college parties and clubs and seen plenty of college girls flashing their tits, but this was very different. This felt like a different world, a world made just for men. I felt like a kid in a candy store. Half-naked women were everywhere, dancing and chatting with men.

I could see it all just standing at the coat check. It was very dark and smoky with strobe lights pulsating to the music's thundering bass. I stood tall and proud as I showed my new I.D. to the bouncer at the door. We were led to a booth by a half naked female usher and my eyes widened. It was amazing to see so many pretty women walking around with their breast and butts totally exposed. They didn't seem to care at all. I foolishly thought that all striper's were junkies with fake breast.

To my surprise, most of them looked like your everyday girl next door. I even thought I recognized a girl that went to high school with me. The D.J. called out the name Snow. She was to go to the main stage to dance. Snow looked a lot like Carrie, a girl who had supposedly gone off to some top college years ago. I made an effort to wave every time I thought she was looking in my direction, but gave up when she didn't respond. I guess I was mistaken.

Our waitress came over and asked for my I.D. "Tonight's your birthday, well, happy birthday. You get a drink on the house." she said. My usual drink was rum and coke, but tonight I wanted something a little more mature. After the guys placed their order's, I asked for a scotch and soda. I continued looking around this dream world, taking it all in. It was just so amazing to me. The waitress arrived with our drinks within minutes.

"Tequila shots? Oh boy!" I said.

Peter gave the toast, wishing me a happy birthday and many more. Before I could get the sting of the first shot down, Luke asked the for another round of tequila shots. I sipped on my scotch while watching the dancers on stage.

It felt really good hanging out with these older guys. By the time our second round of shots came around I was feeling far more relaxed. I decided to ask a question that I'd asked many guy's my age but never any older guys. "Hey, Peter, let me ask you a question," I said leaning into his ear. "This may seem like an odd question but when you see an attractive woman, what goes through your head?"

"Sex," Peter said quickly, laughing at his quick response.

"No, I mean do you ever sort of visualize yourself having sex with her?"

Even though I'd directed my question to Peter, Earl decided to give his two cents.

"Hell yeah, man," he said before Peter could respond.

"Oh, okay," I said, taking a sip from my scotch and soda. I wanted to know if there was a difference in men at different ages.

"All guys constantly fantasize, Josh." Luke said, Joining the conversation.

"It's a natural male ability we all have, enjoy it," Peter added.

"We're visual being's. Women are emotional. They feel, we see." Luke started. "Everyman in here can pull up a woman in our heads that we may have seen a week, month, or year ago, and believe we're having sex with her instantly. It's a man thing. Woman have no idea. Personally, I hope they never know. They probably wouldn't believe it anyway." Luke chuckled after giving his little speech. I sat there for a moment thinking to myself, *I'm all right. Nothings wrong with me.* I washed down my scotch and ordered another. I was really starting to enjoy myself.

Every time a girl passed by our table, one of the guys would either give me a look or ask me if I wanted a dance from them. The D.J. announced a dance finale over the microphone and all of a sudden women started pouring out to the main stage. A couple of them blew kisses toward our booth. I guess Peter, Luke, and Earl may have been here a few times before. The two girls who'd blown kisses came over to our booth shortly after the finale was over. They were awesome, very fit and so damn sexy. Lana and Shyla were their names. They squeezed in to the booth and started taking off their shoes. They weren't bothered at all with me looking at their rock hard nipples. They could tell I was green to the whole strip club experience. They made sure to give me all their sultry eye contact, probably to get me interested in a lap dance. Shyla did a lap dance for Peter and Lana did one for Luke. It was pretty cool watching them go. I was amazed that this stuff was even legal. It was so close to actual sex. We ordered drinks for our new friends as they discussed a little of their personal life. I asked Shyla where the men's room was and she was more than happy to show me, walking me straight there, holding my hand. These girls were so touchy feely. I could see how men could get addicted to this lifestyle.

The reason for the personal escort was so she could ask me for a dance when I got done. "Sure babe. When I return I'd love a dance from you. I'll be right back." I said smiling.

On my return from the men's room, I finally saw why fate sent me. Her name was Sunshine.

Earl had noticed her stepping on to the main stage too. He gave me a nudge in the ribs as I was sliding back into the booth. "Now that's a woman...Wow!" Earl said.

All eye's were on Sunshine as she started her dance. I totally forgot about getting a dance from Shyla. The only dance I wanted would be from Sunshine. She was breath taking. She had long, silky legs, sexy eyes, long brown hair and the most exotic features. She was a golden brown and looked as though she could have been from south America. She was color coordinated from her heels to her earrings.

Wrapped in a yellow T-back style swimsuit, her body became one with the music. Every movement she made was slow and hypnotic. While I was lost in the moment, Sunshine must have felt my stare. She turned in my direction and played with her breast, looking me right in the eyes. I was savoring the moment.

"I think she like you, boy," Earl said, Tapping my shoulder.

"Calm down old man before you have a heart attack." I said. Maybe that would keep him from poking me every time a woman looked my way. He was starting to annoy me a little. Earl defended his self after taking a sip of his drink.

"I was just trying to help you out. You haven't picked a girl to dance for you yet. They don't bite, unless you want them to," he said, smiling.

"Yeah, well I'm picky when it comes to women. I don't want just anyone sitting on my lap and I know one thing, I want her to give my first ever private dance." I said, I pointing to Sunshine who was now finishing up her dance on stage.

"You heard the man. That's the one," Peter said . Lana and Shyla were still at our table. I noticed that they both sort of gave looks of disgust. I was curious why they looked so irritated, so I asked, "What's the problem?"

Shyla didn't hesitate with her response. "Sunshine is a stuck-up bit**." She said with attitude.

"Oh really?" I said

"Yeah! She thinks she's all that," Shyla said, counting her money from her dances.

Sunshine started to leave the stage. Suddenly Lana and Shyla decided they had to go make some money and abruptly left. To me they seemed to be the bitchy ones. They'd made about eighty dollars a piece from Peter and Luke, and drank up a good forty dollars' worth of alcohol. My companions got Sunshine's attention and called her over. She was so polite. She asked how everyone was doing and then asked if she could take a seat. The smell of flower's filled the air as she scooted in next to me. We exchanged pleasantries, while smiling at each other. I was about to compliment her on her dancing when the cocktail waitress came over asking for drinks orders.

"I'll have a fuzzy navel," Sunshine said. She was so damn exotic I couldn't keep my eyes off of her. The D.J. played a love song which must have been Sunshine's favorite, because she whispered in my ear. "This will be the best dance of your life."

She moved the table out a little and pulled me to the edge of the booth. She spread my legs then adjusted herself on my lap. She began rolling and grinding her soft bare butt on my crotch. It was wonderful. It looked as if she was enjoying it as much as I was. It was a great tease show. She could touch me but I couldn't touch her. She would put her breast so close to my mouth I couldn't help but try and kiss them. She reminded that I couldn't by waving her index finger at me and saying no. At times during the dance she would pull her G-string down below her bikini line. It got even harder to contain myself when she opened my legs again and placed her head in my crotch, simulating oral sex. This girl was a professional. This was about the only time I didn't get laid, but almost felt like I did. She did another four songs and I loved every one of them.

"Can I have your telephone number? I'd love to take you out sometime?" I asked after the fifth dance.

"Sorry, I don't give out my number." she said, flashing a sexy smile. "Maybe if we knew each other better."

"I guess I'll have to get to know you better then," I said as I watched her put on her costume top.

"I think I'll see you again, Josh." she said, giving me a wink.

"Something tells me you will," I said. As I watched her walk away. She didn't know it but the two of us would get to know each other much sooner than we thought.

• • • • •

It was almost two o'clock in the morning when I staggered through the front door. I went directly to the medicine cabinet upstairs and swallowed some aspirin, hoping It would help me wake up without a headache. My body slammed onto my bed like a ton of bricks. I fell asleep fully clothed.

• • • • •

"Joshua! Joshua! Wake up!" My mother was bellowing from the bottom of the stairs. I rolled over to one side, wrapping my pillow around my head, hoping to drown out her voice. I heard her stomping her way up to my bedroom door, second's later she was pounding on my door.

"Josh, get up. you have company." My mother loved to wake me up after a night out. She would have yelled whether I had company or not. I had a banging headache but no nausea.

"I'll be right down," I said, yelling at my bedroom door.

I could hear my mother walking away mumbling something under her breath. I finally got off my bed and went to my bathroom to wash-up. I felt like shit. I started down the stairs where I was met near the bottom by my mother. "What the hell is wrong with you?" She said with a angry frown. Every time my mother had this kind of attitude it was hard to bite my tongue. I didn't want to say something I would regret later. It was her house, her rules.

"Nothing," I finally said, holding the side of my head. She rolled her eyes and shoved a gift into my hands. "What's this?" I said, smiling.

"It was your birthday yesterday, wasn't it?" she asked.

"Yeah," I said, smiling at her.

"Well, do the math, genius." she walked away before I could say thank you, so I yelled it out after her. I wanted her to know that her gift was appreciated, but it was no use.

Instantly she switched on her *ignore* mode, just to make me feel guilty for snapping at her. As soon as I turned from the foyer into the kitchen I saw Amy having coffee at the kitchen table.

"Are you okay?" she asked. "you look a little out of it."

"Yeah, babe, I'm alright. Just a little headache, that's all." I walked over and gave her a kiss and a hug. "I missed you, babe."

"Aw, well I'm back to take care of you." she said, looking into my eyes.

I wasn't sure if it was the hangover or the lingering picture of Sunshine in my head that made Amy appear so average-looking to me. Amy just wasn't as mystifying as I thought after seeing someone like Sunshine.

"So what happened while I was gone?" she asked.

"I spent some time with the guys... Just hanging out a little. Nothing special," I said, pretending I had a boring night. I decided right on the spot that this was the perfect time to play up the "move in together idea." I gazed out the kitchen window few moments, readying my game face.

"Babe, I've got to tell you, I've been thinking about moving out. My parents don't respect me. Living here is just becoming a bit too much."

I placed my head in my hands and took a deep breath. I exhaled a few seconds later, acting as though the thought was depressing to me. I was playing up the drama, going for Amy's heart strings like a master actor. "They can't give me five minutes to myself without finding something to argue about. I'm sick of it. Something seems to be pushing us together. What I'm saying is that I'd like to be with you and only you. If we were ever to get…"

I stopped right there to let her natural curiosity take over and for her to think about what I'd just said. I put my hand on her knee. "Well, we haven't really known each other long enough for me to be talking like this. I hope I'm not making you feel uncomfortable."

"No, not at all," she said, listening intently.

"It's just that I can't stop thinking about you." The way I spoke and looked at her would have made even me believe I was sincere, so it had to be working on her. Her face was full of concern, I stole a glance at her out of the corner of my eye. It was a Performance worthy of an Oscar. Women tend to think that men can't act as well as they can. Remember one thing, men invented acting. We do it everyday in way's women haven't even discovered yet.

I could feel that I was minutes away from hearing what I wanted to hear. I could see me living in her condo with all the sex I wanted any time. I asked her to join me in the family room. I took her hand and lead her. I turned on the affection while we sat there pretending to watch television. I snuggled next to her, giving her soft butterfly kisses up and down her neck. Then I suddenly realized that I'd been so caught up in my plan that I totally forgot to ask about her trip. "So, how was your trip?" I asked in a soft whisper.

She immediately started to rattle off details and events almost nonstop. I tried my best to appear interested by staring at her lips. It's a tactic we men use a lot. Usually we nod intermittently and look at the woman's face, moving our gaze from lips to eyes, lips to eyes. She finally paused and started to say what I had been waiting to hear.

She began with a serious look. "Josh, I can tell you care about me, I feel the same way about you. I think you and I could be the perfect couple. I'd really like you to move in with me." She held her index finger up to my lips, before I could begin my fake protest. "Before you say no, I know couples that haven't known each other half as long as we have and they live together and are doing fine. I'm not trying to rush you into anything. But I want us to be together all the time."

I took her soft hand in mine and caressed her palm against my face. "Let me think about it a little," I said smiling and then resting my head on her shoulder.

She had fallen for my bullshit. I decided to take her to lunch so I could fill her head with more fantasies. I wanted to play it slow. She knew sooner or later I was going to leave my mothers house. Soon she'd almost demand that I move in because she'd worry about me cheating if I got a place of my own.

• • • • •

A couple of months passed and I still hadn't moved out of my parent's house. I was taking my time. My parents would ask me periodically about my relationship with Amy, asking me how it was going. My answer was almost always the same. "I don't know..." or I'd find some other vague response. My mother wanted more information but I liked to keep her guessing. "Mom, I have no plans of moving in with her. I just like spending some nights away from home," I'd say.

"Joshua, that's a grown woman your dealing with, not some silly college girl. I think she's very serious about your relationship. Don't play games with her because if you break her heart, she may not take it so easy. You cant go around leading women along. It's wrong. Think about their feelings for once in your life." My mother is so sweet, always caring about other people's feelings. Like most women, she had one problem: *She doesn't understand men.* Her words went in one ear and out the other.

Looking back, my mother's wisdom could have paid off if only I'd listened. I led Amy along like she had a ring in her nose. Our relationship wasn't bad. We had good sex almost every time we were together. It started out great, but she wasn't big on oral sex at all, something we guys like to have from time to time. It gives us a feeling of control over the woman. This is something you wont hear any man admit, but that's the real reason behind it. We love to feel that we are dominant and in control.

Amy pampered the hell out of me anytime I stayed at her condo. Some mornings she would have my clothes ironed and breakfast for me. She would made the best cappuccino. If I went to her home after work, I would walk in to find the table set with my dinner waiting. After dinner, we'd watch some television or have sex and sometimes we'd do both. We had sex all over that condo.

I kept a small wardrobe at Amy's place. I figured if we had a fight or things didn't work out, it would be easy to load up and leave. Leaving most of my stuff at my parents home was an advantage. If I realized I'd left something at my parents home I needed. Amy would volunteer to go buy something just like it. It was all sort of a practice run to see what the married life would be like.

Amy received word that she was to head store promotion's for a new cosmetic line that was soon coming to shopping malls across the U.S. It was a really big deal for Her. She couldn't stop talking about it. New opportunties would be coming her way as well as a chance to make a lot more money.

The new line was to be set up and ready by Friday morning. Amy was running around like mad trying to make sure everything went smoothly. Fifty tester units she ordered never made it to the malls; instead they were shipped to her home address. She couldn't be in two places at once so she called her sister who was familiar with the project and asked her if she could help her out by picking up the units and dropping them off at the mall near her house. I wasn't much help to her. To this day, I still don't even know what a tester unit is.

Amy explained that her sister would be by to pick up the units and to please let her in. Since I had never heard much about her sister, I was kind of excited to meet her. I decided to work out a bit to look pumped up just incase she was good looking.

One of men's big fantasy's is to have sex with sisters. It's right up there with our fantasy about twins. I can't tell you why this is such a big fantasy within our world, it just is and I wasn't about to lose my chance at a possible sister threesome. We also have the girlfriend with girlfriend fantasy. Believe me when I tell you. If you have ever felt your boyfriend or husband may have feelings for your best friend, your right on the money. The truth is it run's through his head more times then you could imagine.

● ● ● ● ●

The door bell rang while I was doing a set of pushup's. I went to the door with nothing on but shorts and socks. My hair was perfect and my chest was nice and buffed.

" Hi! You must be Lydia." I knew I had caught her of guard because she paused before shaking my extended hand. She introduced herself and walked in. She was a little older than Amy but just as cute. "Your far better looking than I thought you would be," I said, testing the waters.

"Thank you," she said, Paying me no mind. "This line is gonna drive Amy crazy."

"Yeah, she's so into it. I'm happy to see her doing her thing," I said.

"Shortcake, shortcake, where's my shortcake," Lydia said softly. I stood there wondering what the hell she was doing.

"What's shortcake?" I asked. "A pet? Amy's doesn't own a pet."

"No, silly that's my nickname for Jaime. I haven't seen her in months. Is she here?" she asked.

I was still lost. Lydia could tell from my blank expression, so she tried to help me out. "Amy's daughter. The blank look turned into surprise.

"You didn't know? Okay, I think I should get the box now. Lydia grabbed the box of the kitchen table and was hurrying to the door. "Nice to have met you, Josh." I didn't say anything because I was in complete shock.

I couldn't believe Amy had lied to me all this time. What the hell could she be thinking. How in the world could a mother keep a secret like that? I was dumbfounded. Maybe she thought in time I'd change my feelings about children. Deciding to keep quiet, knowing that if she was to mention her daughter up front she would have no chance with me. I would have preferred to be told up front.

Now I could never ever trust her. I felt like packing it all in. I wanted to say "to hell with it." Still, I had to cool down and think. If I didn't, I could lose out on this easy life style. It was time to think before I acted.

· · · · ·

Later that evening Amy walked through the door and greeting me with a kiss. "I know you don't mind carryout, so I picked up some on the way in. Mmmm, Chinese," she said, opening the bag of food, inhaling the aroma. Then she asked the question I'd been waiting to hear. "Did my sister come by? She never called to tell me if he got the unit's or not. I was bouncing all over the place. I had such a busy day sweetie." I decided to stop her right in her tracks. If I hadn't she would have talked for hours. She started pulling plates from the cabinet.

"Amy, I thought I made it very clear early in our relationship that I didn't want anything to do with kids. I guess being honest was just a little too much for you to handle." I said with a stern look. I poured myself a glass of wine and stood there watching her slowly sit down at the dining room table. She didn't say anything. "I don't like being lied to, Amy."

"What are you talking about?" she said, pretending not to know.

"What do you think? I asked you about that picture." I pointed to the coffee table.

"I asked you about the kids' blanket, but you decided to lie."

"You're right, you did that, but you never asked me if I had any children."

"I see what's going on. We're having a god damn play on words now. You know what I meant when I asked questions like that. Don't play the airhead with me, Amy"

"No, you asked certain questions and I answered you. Don't get so damn bent out of shape. if you want direct answers, ask direct question." She had the nerve to get snippy with me. The arguing went back and fourth for minutes. By the time it all ended, I agreed that I would ask direct questions from then on. I guess I'd finally got a taste of my own medicine.

The following morning we both apologized. Amy suddenly wanted to talk about her daughter. Summer vacation was coming up and Jaime would stay the entire summer. I decided to give it a try. One child couldn't be that bad.

Two months later Jaime Arrived. Jaime had dishwater blonde hair and some of the biggest glasses I'd ever seen on a child. She wasn't the cutest child I'd ever seen. I could see why Amy never bragged about her. Amy's mother was nice. She was very elegant yet stylish and carried herself like she was a royal. I found myself being treated like a family man, a position for which I wasn't ready for. I had a child in my life, a woman who treated me like a husband, and a job that I feared would end up being the only reason to get up everyday. I wasn't ready for that. I'd already started to feel a bit bored with Amy and the last thing I needed was a complete family to make my like even more drab.

The guys had given me all kinds of advise about my situation. For the most part, I got, go with the flow. "Just stay with Amy and get another woman or two on the Side." they advised me. Some said I was in a great postion. They believed a woman with a child would stay with you no matter what, because they're stuck. They said as women get older they give up and turn their heads when a man starts to cheat. They said to just act as though I liked her child and she'd never let me go. I'd be set for life, but that's what I was afraid of. I knew it wouldn't be long before she'd start thinking about marriage if she hadn't been already. I got a little advise on how to handle that from Peter.

"If it comes up, Josh, just stall. Say you want to finish school or something. You can always buy her a "stall ring" for her birthday or something. It'll be nothing more than a friendship ring to you, but to woman a diamond ring is the perfect item to buy time. Put a ring on a womans finger and you can get away with almost anything. Trust me. Your in a great position, Josh. Use it to your advantage."

A lot of what the guys said made sense, all I had to do was play her along. I could be sweet to her and her daughter and live my other life behind the scenes like most men do.

I decided to be the perfect guy. It was a bit tough for me getting use to Jaime. She was such a curious child. She always wanted to know what I was doing and where I was going. If I was reading a book or a newspaper she'd ask what I was doing. I had to take a break every know and then. I'd disappear for hour's at a time. Kid's just weren't my thing.

It wasn't long before Jaime's summer vacation would be over and she'd have to go back to that private school near her grandmothers house. I poured on the fatherly love the closer she got to departure. Amy loved me for it. Everything the guys told me was starting to happen.

Jaime's departure day soon arrived. Amy was going to drive her mother and daughter to the airport. I told Jaime I was going to miss her and couldn't wait for her return. We shared kisses and hugs, then they were out the door and on their way. I decided to go for a workout. I put on my work-out clothes and was off to the communities gym facilities.

I often enjoyed an early morning workout. I had just got done with the stair climber and started setting my weight on the bench press when I heard a soft female voice ask, "You need a spotter? That's a lot of weight." Standing in the doorway was a lady with a knock-out figure in some of the tiniest short's I'd ever seen.

"Wow! Where did you come from?" I said with surprise. "I thought I was here alone."

"I've been here for a bit, cycling in the bike room. Hi! I'm Rebecca," She said, extending her hand.

"I'm Joshua. Nice to meet you." I took her hand with a soft touch, checking out her body the entire time. Right away my man thoughts kicked in. *I think I just found myself a second girlfriend.*

• • • • •

We men are always fishing… Always, especially if the man is confident. It's something we don't even think about, we just do it. Married or not, we always have our eye out for something new.

"Do you mind if I workout with you?" She asked.

"Not at all. I could use the company."

"Your in pretty good shape, do you come over here often?"

"Every now and then. I usually work out at home with the basic's, push-ups and sit-ups, but sometimes I feel like lifting so I come here," I said, loading weight plates on the bench press.

"I'm new to this area. I got transferred here a week ago. I think I'm going to like It here," she said, giving me the eye.

"Hang around me and I know you will," I said, flirting. "Ready? please don't let this fall on me."

I laid on the bench and started a set. she was standing above my head spotting me. It was so hard to concentrate because I kept visualizing her standing there with her breast out. The male mind, always working. I could tell that she was interested in getting to know me a lot better. Rebecca and I worked out and chatted for almost an hour, flirting the entire time. It was hard because anytime she'd touch me or get really close to me no matter how briefly, I'd get aroused and would have to think of something else to keep my mind off of sex. I give her a back massage after our work-out to let her know I was ready to play. My massage naturally went all the way down to her butt crack. After all, a guy's gotta try.

"We'll, Josh, I must be going. It was nice to meet you. I hope to see you again tomorrow."

"I'll be here," I said. "It was nice." I took her hand and kissed it. Then looked in her eye's. She looked right back and bit her lip a little to tell me she had plans for me too. I was being given the green light and the best thing was she lived in the same condo complex. I was dying for some new action, but I had to be careful. Things with Amy and me were going pretty well and I could really screw things up if she was to find out I'd been screwing her neighbor. I'd just keep Rebecca around just to see what would happen between us. Hopefully a new addiction to my secret panty collection.

The day was starting out perfectly. Jaime was gone and I didn't have to participate in tea parties and board games for at least eight months. To make things even better Amy would be leaving for Chicago in just three days on business. It would be the perfect time for me to have some personal time to myself. I had plans already set. I figured it was time to give Sunshine a visit.

• • • • •

I dropped Amy at the airport an hour early, kissed her on the cheek, and told her I couldn't wait for her to return so we could have time alone. I was all smiles as I drove to the topless bar where I'd first laid eyes on Sunshine. I arrived much earlier than I did the first time. It felt a little weird going into a bar at five o'clock in the afternoon. The bar wasn't as busy as it was the night of my birthday. The afternoon clientele was different as well. It was odd to see so many business men there in their Suit's and ties. *So this is where they go after work,* I thought. There were many men drinking and eating finger foods with some of the dancers. I walked around the bar, keeping an eye out for Sunshine. I spotted her sitting with another girl sipping on a cocktail.

"Hi," I said, winking and sliding into the booth. "How're you doing."

"Hey, you were here for your birthday a while ago, I think," she said, trying to remember.

"You remembered. Aww, I feel special." I was shocked. That's was a good sign because there had to be guys coming in all the time for parties and such. "Josh." I said pointing to myself.

"I remember you. Your friend Peter comes in sometimes." Sunshine's friend decided to go do a dance and left.

"She a friend of yours?" I asked.

"Sort of… we were just killing time." She started to put on her lips stick and shoes like she was leaving.

"Where are you going?" I asked. I wanted her to stay so I could get to know her a little.

"Gonna try and squeeze some money out of these cheap a** regular's."

"Yeah, I saw that this crowd was a lot different from the late night crowd," I said.

"These guy all have their favorite girls. Some of the girls have relationships with them so it's harder to get dances."

"I see, well maybe this will help out." I put my hand into my pocket and pulled out two hundred dollar bills and pushed them in front of Sunshine. "If you promise to keep my company."

Wide-eyed and grinning, she took the money and said, thanks."

The waitress took our order as we continued to chat. I'd convinced her to leave work and join me for a bite to eat. We decided to go to a Italian restraunt, because she mentioned it was her favorite type of food. It felt odd having such a head turner as my date. This girl was a stunner. I noticed people constantly staring at us, stopping their conversations mid-sentence just to take a look. We placed our order and had light conversation.

She told me that her real name was Gabrielle and that her friends call her Gabby. She was very easy to talk to and a very good listener. I began telling her about my home life and my problems with Amy, how Amy lied to me about her daughter and how I felt tricked into playing the role of a stepfather. Gabrielle agreed with me that Amy should have been upfront with her daughter, but explained that when a woman likes a man they are very afraid of losing him.

Sometimes they'll do extreme things to keep him until they figure things out. "Everyone deserves a second chance," She said. "If it weren't for second chances we'd all be screwed." This made me wonder why a bright beautiful girl would decideon taking her clothes off for a living. I found out that Gabrielle had come from Mexico. She'd tried to attend college, but couldn't keep up. She had a friend who worked as a stripper that eventually introduced her to it. The money was good so she decided to do it and had been doing it for the last three years.

"I'm just working and saving my money until I decide what I want to do next," she said. I was really enjoying Gabrielle's company. I was beginning to understand why those businessmen hung out with the girls at the bar. Sometimes we men just need female company to talk about things we can't with our girlfriends or wives.

Hours later I drove her back to the bar. She decided to just take the rest of the night off and asked if I wanted to hang out with her at her house. *This was music to my ears.*

A short time later we arrived at her apartment complex. I started to see she wanted what I wanted, companionship. She enjoyed my company just as much as I enjoyed hers. That night we watched movies, popped microwave popcorn and snuggled together on her couch. It was so nice. When the clock struck eleven o'clock., I decided to call it a night.

Gabrielle had gotten a case of the yawns, but before I left we made plans to go to a movie. I got her telephone number and gave her a kiss on the lips. Walking down to my car, all I could think about was her soft lips and her sweet smell.

That afternoon after giving her time to sleep, I decided to give her a call to see if she still wanted to hang out. She decided to take a day off and spend the day with me. I can't really pen point why I was so interested in her. I knew I loved her exotic looks and conversation, but I also had a feeling that I just liked being seen with her.

I think a lot of men do this. To be honest I just love beauty and there's nothing more beautiful than women in my opinion.

A few hours later I picked her up and we went to the mall because she needed to buy some new clothes. It felt like the entire mall was watching us. I was living a bit dangerously seeing how Amy had friends at malls all over town. We later had lunch outside at a trendy café. Her conversation and energy was just great. We started getting closer and closer, touching and even holding hands from time to time. It was a warm day so we decided to skip the movie and went to a park near the lake. We just ate ice cream and watching the boats sailing around. I was having such a good time I hated to think about the downside. Amy would was coming home tomorrow. I let Gabby know we wouldn't be able to hang out as much as we have been. She understood, saying there was no crime in enjoying each others company.

I told her I'd come and see her at work from time to time, "Sounds good to me," she said.

About an hour later we pulled into her apartment and sat in the car talking for a moment.

"I really like you, Gabby." I gave her a serious look. I motioned with my finger for her to come closer and gave her a kiss that lasted several seconds. She didn't say a word after the kiss, just flashed her beautiful smile at me and got out. *Oh boy!* I thought. I've got a stripper for a girlfriend, but now what am I going to do about Amy?

Chapter 4

NO LEASH

I kept my promise to Gabrielle, visiting her as much as possible over the next two years. Lucky for me, many of those visits lead to sex. Gabrielle was very open- minded about the entire thing. It was a odd relationship, but it worked. Gabrielle knew I didn't really know what I wanted in a relationship, so she gave me all the time I needed. We were friends before sexual partners, so there was no pressure for commitment.

Amy, on the other hand, was pushing more and more as time passed for a solid commitment. Jaime had begun to call me "Daddy" and Amy encouraged it. I wasn't at all happy about it. I think she figured that she would push me as much as possible, hoping Jaime would pull on my heart strings and make me commit, but all It did was make me want to escape.

One day, I sat Amy down and explained to her that I wasn't Jaime's father and wasn't trying to be. Amy got so upset with me that she threw me out. We ended up back together just a week later. It was such a confusing time for me. I liked Amy and I liked Gabby as well, but didn't actually want full commitment to either of them. Amy and I went through break-ups and make-ups so many times that I started getting use to it.

Since I didn't know what to do but still enjoyed Amy. I decided to pull out *plan B,* which was to lead her in to believing that we would be married one day. I waited for her birthday and surprised her with a half-carrot diamond ring. It worked like magic. She behaved as though she had won a car on a game show or something. She cried, and laughed at the same time. It actually made me feel good to do it. I hoped it would buy me a little more time.

In the meantime Rebecca and I continued to meet to workout together, in more ways than one. It was nothing serious. We had sex only three times in the course of a year, mainly because, she'd only have sex if we used a condom. Sure, it's good to be safe, I understand that, but I believe if you have to wear a condom, you probably shouldn't be having sex in the first place. No one likes condoms. Let's face it, The only thing having a good time during sex is the condom. I've always been one who wants the total experience.

At work, my sales continued to grow. My commissions were getting bigger and bigger, partly because my regular customers who liked me would send their frends to me. They liked my openess. I'd discuss everything with my customers, the most common subject being women. It's amazing how easily it is to bond with another male, all you have to do is discuss women.

Then it happened. I had relaxed too much and gotten a little sloppy. I started calling Gabrielle from Amy's house when she wasn't home, which turned out to be a big mistake.

I had a funny feeling when Amy called me at work and said come on by when I got off. She had a certain sound in her voice, I knew something was going on. After work I went on over to Amy's. When I came through the door, I was surprised to see Amy holding her telephone bill. There were number highlighted in yellow. I prayed she hadn't called the number. I tried to act like I didn't even notice she was holding it.

"Hi babe," I said try to kiss her. Amy ignored me and threw the bill at me as I walked in. "What was that for?" I asked.

"F*** you, Josh!" I had never heard Amy curse like that. This was serious. "I talked to your f***ing whore."

"What are you talking about?" I asked, trying to play dumb.

"I'm talking about this, your whore, who knows your name and knows where I live." Amy's face was so red I was starting to get a little nervous. "Have you been screwing this b**** in my house?"

"This has to be a mistake," I said. The next thing I felt was my ear ringing and my face stinging from the biggest slap I'd ever felt. Stunned, I stepped back to compose myself. "What the hell is wrong with you?" I said, getting angry.

"You're a piece of sh**!" Amy screamed, with tears in her eyes.

I was trying to explain again when she drew back and gave me a heavy slap to my nose and eye. I immediately grabbed my face. "You f***," I said, noticing the blood on my hand.

Amy started towards the kitchen and I followed behind her. She went right to the silverware drawers and I knew this was gonna turn very bad. She was crying so hard her breath was shallow. She was enraged. I turned and started fast walking to the door.

"I hate you!" Amy screamed, coming towards me with a kitchen knife. *Oh sh**!* heart pounding, I darted out the door and to my car. I couldn't get my keys into the ignition fast enough. She was really going to stab me. "That was crazy!" I said out loud, driving to my mothers house. My nose was stuffy and still bleeding.

My mother knew something was wrong by the blood on my shirt when I walked through the front door. "What happened?" she asked, obviously concerned.

"Uh, Amy and I got into a fight," I said, struggling to breath through my very bloody nose. I headed straight for the bathroom to rinse the blood from my nose. "Thank God it isn't broken," I said. I looked in the mirror and gingerly wiggled my Nose, testing it for a break.

After telling my mother the story, I called Gabrielle to let her know what had happened. Gabrielle said that she had just got out of the shower when Amy called her.

"She immediately asked who I was and when I didn't tell her, Amy called me all kinds of names, so I fired back. I cussed at her and then told her all about our sex life to piss her off."

Gabby explained that she hadn't wanted to hurt me, only Amy for swearing at her. Gabrielle was very apologetic but also told me it was time for me to decide because she didn't need drama in her life.

I apologized to Gabrielle and told her that Amy was definitely out of the picture. We had been talking for almost an hour when the telephone beeped with a call waiting. I switched over to take the call. It was Amy, crying and apologizing. She sounded so sad and pitiful on the telephone. I had never seen this side of her. Once again I was confused and caught between what I wanted and what I thought I needed.

Amy said, if I could forgive her, she could forgive me. I felt so sorry for her, I told her, "Let me think about it."

I couldn't believe the chain of events. I was the one who had screwed up. Maybe Amy somehow thought that it was her fault that I was cheating. It was just like so many men had told me. The longer your with a woman, the more lenient they will become. I had gotten caught cheating and she was ready to forgive me in a matter of hours. She begged me to come back to her house that night. She was very worried about my nose.

There was no way I was going back there after her emotional outburst and attack. I told her that we would talk about it later and hung up the phone. I must have talked to Amy for too long because when I switched the telephone line back to Gabrielle she had already hung up. I immediately called Gabby, apologizing for having her on hold for so long. I told her that it was a business call for my stepfather. Gabrielle had no idea it was Amy who had called. I told Gabrielle that it was time for me to take a break and find out what I wanted to do.

• • • • •

In the days that followed I decied to work on getting my own place so I could do whatever I damn well pleased. I Bounced between Amy's condo and Gabby's place for the months all the while saving and planning my next move. My mother thought I was crazy to see Amy again, but I liked her company and the sex got much better. It was also exciting to have a girlfriend that was so unpredictable.

At work things got a lot more serious. The company had begun to weed out the older employees to make room for new people. There were changes at the corporate level as well, word was that they were trimming the fat because overall sales in the company were falling sharply, there was even talk of the company being sold to a bigger competitor if things didn't improve. I wasn't in any danger, because I always made top three in sales each month. Most of the other employees at our store were starting to worry, except Peter, who wasn't worried at all, as a matter of fact, he grew more reckless. I pulled into the parking lot one morning and noticed Peter sitting in his car with a young lady who wasn't his wife. I decided to watch for a little bit to see what he was up to. Minutes later the lady got out of Peters car and into hers. it was Jennifer Voss, the regional manager's daughter. Peter had no shame. She was far too young for him. Peter had mentioned to us several times that he wanted to screw her, but I never thought he'd get the opportunity. I bet her father Glen, had no idea what was going on. I immediately saw a golden opportunity in this for me.

Peter knew I had been watching because as soon as we opened the store, he let me know in a subtle way that I had seen nothing. I played along, letting him know that my mouth was shut, for the time being anyway. I don't like to be intimidated or threatened. I'd just keep this secret to myself until the time was right.

Time started to fly by. My social life had begun to smooth out. I started hanging out at clubs and meeting new women. Gabrielle was still in my life, as well as Amy, who I still considered my girlfriend. I started taking full advantage of her. I'd call her only when I felt like it. I had become even more promiscuous. Sometimes she'd find out about my escapades, but would do little or nothing about it. Sometimes she'd confront me, raising her voice, but that's about as heated as it would become. I'd just storm out, later returning to a full apology.

She'd begun sneaking around, trying to spy on me. I think I was beginning to really drive her a little crazy. There were times when I'd wake up at night and see her going through my pockets. If we went somewhere together and she was in my passenger seat, she'd ask, "Who's been sitting here? This seat wasn't like this last time I sat here." I'd just make up something quick, like 'I took a coworker home' or 'I went out for a drink with one of the guys and I drove.' She always knew I was lying, but she just liked to try to catch me.

Poor Amy was starting to lose it. I'd test her to see just how far I could go. I'd make up things and act like I was pissed off with her just to see what she would do. Instead of swearing back or getting mad, now she'd stay quiet, later buying me a gift or cooking something special for me. Sometimes she'd even wear lingerie for me, something she never ever did before. I had her under complete control.

Looking back, it was a horrible thing to do to her. I think far too many women fall into relationships like this. Once a woman turns a blind eye to our misbehavior, we men have total control in the relationship and when a relationship has no balance, it's over.

• • • • •

The secret I'd been keeping about Peter and Jennifer would soon come into play. There were manager training classes being given in Chicago. Peter, of all People, recommended me to participate. All those selected would go to meet and greet all the top bosses and receive information about the management training program. Basically the big bosses wanted to see who to pick for a shot at management positions. This was the perfect opportunity for me to meet with Glen Voss. I'd met him a couple of times before, but this time I actually had something to talk about.

I arrived in Chicago on an early Tuesday morning. I could barely keep my eyes open as we sat through rounds of introductions and pep talks. I made sure to applaud between my long yawns. After the meeting everyone hung around to mingle and kiss up a little. I spotted Glen and waited patiently for my chance. After a little general conversation, Glen finally asked the question I'd been waiting on.

"So Joshua, how are things going at the store?" I took a deep breath to relax and put on a demeanor or concern.

"Well, I'm glad you asked, Sir. To be honest with you, there's a lot of things that shouldn't be going on."

"Such as?" he asked, urging me to continue.

I moved closer to Glen's ear. "I have knowledge of management having sex with employees," I said in a whisper.

"Things like that happen, Joshua. That's not a problem unless it interupts job performance." We walked to an unoccupied table and sat down to continue our conversation.

"No, sir, I don't think I'm making my self clear. Our store manager, Peter, has had sex with a female employee inside our store."

Glen didn't look happy at all with the news. He took a drink from his bottle of water. "Are you sure Josh?" he asked. becoming very serious.

"Yes sir, I wouldn't lie about something like that. Actually, I witnessed it. I was a little shocked because Peter is a married man. Management is suppose to set an example for others to follow. I don't think that's a very good one."

Now that I had his attention, I decided to drop the big one. "Mr. Voss, there's something else I think you should know. Not long ago I saw Peter in our parking lot sitting with a young lady in his car who looked a lot like your daughter Jennifer."

Glen turned red and just sat quiet for a few moments, like he was trying to calm himself. "To be very honest, Glen mentioned a few times that he wanted to get to know Jennifer a lot better ever since she became district supervisor for the company. I'm not looking to get anyone in trouble, but I thought this was something that you should be aware of." It was difficult to tell what Glen was thinking. He could have been in shock, but I couldn't tell.

"Thank you, Joshua. This conversation never happened." he said, looking me straight in the eye. "I'll talk to you soon."

Glen stood up and in a few big strides was gone. I wasn't sure if he was mad at me for spilling the beans or furious with Peter. He was a hard man to get a read.

I didn't feel bad about what I'd done. I had an opportunity and I took it. What man wouldn't? I decided to stick around and rub elbows with the bosses. I talked with managers and directors from all over the company. There were a couple of female bosses and manager trainees as well. We chatted in the meeting room's for almost an hour eating finger foods and talking about business and technology. Most of these guys were pretty easy to get along with.

After the ladies left, they dropped their facades and the man talk began. The usual conversations about sports and women started once we all got a bit more comfortable with each other. This is the typical order of conversation when ever you have a bunch of guys together, Sports arguments and female jokes as usual. I got on the elevator to leave with Tom Kemp and Bill Smit, two bosses I'd spent most of my time with all morning and afternoon. They were arguing about female celebrities as we boarded the elevator. The argument soon halted when the elevator door opened on the next floor. We all moved to the side as two women got on. I was the first to speak.

"Good afternoon." They nodded and smiled.

"Hello," Bill said. The elevator stopped three floor's later. "Have a good afternoon." Bill said, as they got off.

Our conversation went directly to man talk as soon as the elevator door closed behind them. Bill nudged Tom's elbow. "How did you like those two? That redhead had a body made for one thing." Bill said, grinning. "I bet shes a little vacuum. She can clean this dirty carpet anytime." Bill said, trying to whisper.

"I liked the breast on the other one. They made me thiroty." Tom oaid. I started to chuckle. "You like that, huh Josh?" bill asked.

"Here's one for you. How do you turn a dishwasher into a snowblower?" Bill asked.

"No idea." I said.

"Give the bi*** a Shovel," Bill said, laughing.

I was a little surpised to see my bosses open up so early on. We men have these types conversations all the time, but for some reason I didn't expect for them to show their real personalities so fast. I figured I must have really fit in for them to open up so quickly.

I decided to catch an early fight out. I wanted to get home so I could take Gabrielle out for lunch the next day. I arrived home late in the evening and went straight to sleep. I called her early the next morning but the telephone just rang. Lately it seemed as though Gabrielle had been purposely distancing herself from me. When ever I called and left a message she wouldn't get back to me. The last couple of times I went to the bar to see her, she pretended to be too busy. I scratched my head wondering what was going on.

I finally tracked her down doing a double shift at the bar. After a few attempts at getting her attention, she finally sat down with me. "What is it Josh?" she asked.

"Baby, whats wrong with you? You been avoiding me for weeks," I took her hand and held it. "did I do something wrong?"

"I deserve more. Our relationship is going nowhere," She s aid. "You've had more than enough time to get figure out what you want in your life. I don't have time to waste. I'm not getting any younger."

"Baby, listen… I love everything about you. I don't want to lose you. To be honest, I'd love to marry you someday. I just need to get some money together first." I never meant to say "marry," it just poped out. I'm actually glad it did because, her entire attitude changed for the better. Ah, marriage… The magic word. What woman doesn't like to hear it?

"You have two weeks to make a decision, Josh. Two weeks. I have to go." *Wow, an ultimatum!* I had to give Gabrielle credit. She wasn't messing around with me. She knew that a man will drag his feet as long as possible. I think working in a topless bar taught her a few things about men. Guys had to be feeding her lies constantly.

• • • • •

The following week I walked into work and knew something was wrong. Almost everyone in the store was quiet as a mouse. I was immediately given the news. Peter had been fired. My little conversation with Glen in Chicago had to be the big reason why. After clocking in Earl approached me looking very nervous. "Hey josh, the boss wants to see you."

"I just heard Peter got fired." I said confused.

"No, The big boss, Glen Voss. He's upstairs."

"Oh!" I said, catching on. I went to the men's room to check my face and mentally prepare myself. *Ok Josh, let's do this.*

I knocked on the door and entered what was formerly Peter's office.

"Hi Joshua, have a seat," Mr. Voss said. He seemed to be in a good mood.

"Thank you, sir," I said.

"Fresh coffee's is over there if you want," Glen said, pointing to the coffee maker near the window.

"No thank you."

"Joshua, it's seems as though everyone is running this store except the , managers. You're opening the store from time to time and that's not even your responsibility. So I've decided to help this store get back to normal." He took a sip of his coffee and then began again. "I've had a chance to look at your performance record. You appear to be a very responsible young man. You haven't ever called in sick and your never late."

"Thank you, sir"

"No, thank you Joshua," he said with a big smile. "What did you think about the manager's meeting in Chicago?"

"Well sir, it answered a lot of questions I had about the company. I'm very interested in becoming a manager and helping the company as best as I can. I'd love some hands on experience in the manager position someday," I said, feeling as confident as ever.

"Call me Glen. I like you, Josh. I think I'll stick with the decision Peter made before his resignation to make you an assistant manager."

I couldn't believe my ears. I stood up to shake Glen's hand. "Thank you very much sir. You wont regret it. I promise."

Glen went on telling me about the salary and the bonus program, which was very nice. I would now be making almost double and still have the opportunity to sell. Amy could kiss my butt goodbye. I could now afford a great place of my own and have plenty of cash left for my savings accounts. Sure, I could have long gotten a place of my own long before, but I wanted to have a beautiful place. Now I finally had the chance.

Not everyone at work was happy about my promotion. The older employees that had been there for years practically had heart attacks after learning of my promotion. That inside information I gave Glen was the big reason for the promotion. With out it I would probably still be stocking shelves and selling merchandise. Glen and I never once discussed that I told him in Chicago. When a man looks you straight in the eye's and say's this never happened, it didn't. I learned this long ago. Men keep many secrets like this between them and take it to their graves. It's the foundation of the male code. Women can't seem to hold secrets at all. The ability to help each other come up in society and keep secrets is why we men have always kept control of society and the women in it.

• • • • •

I started treating Gabrielle like she was a real girlfriend, buying her flowers and chocolates. taking her out to clubs and lounges, really enjoying her. As for Amy, I still saw her, but rarely. I moved almost all my clothes back to my mothers house. I was stepping out of Amy's life more and more with each passing day.

All of a sudden, things got weird. I started receiving telephone calls at work, but when I would say hello they would just hang up. My suspicions were confirmed the day I got an announcement over the intercom for me to pick up line two.

"Hello, this is Joshua. How can I help you?"

"Are you leaving me for that whore?" Amy screamed into the phone.

"I don't have time for your games, Amy. Make this your last time calling me. Do you understand? It's over. *O.V.E.R.* Got it?" I meant every word. I just didn't care anymore.

"Answer me, you son of a bit**!" she screamed. "Answer me!"

I just hung up the phone.

• • • • •

Three days later, I was in Glens office discussing the upcoming annual electronics convention held in Las Vegas when Mike Reed started knocking on the office door. "Yes come in," said Glen.

"Excuse me guys, but I think Josh needs to see this," said Mike. He seemed a little shaken by something.

"What's wrong Mike?" I said, following him. He didn't say a word. "Whats going on?" I asked as he lead me outside to the parking lot.

"Oh my god!" I said, as I walked up to my destroyed Acura. All four of my tires were flat and there was black paint slashed across it's hood, roof and driver's side door. "*F***!*" I yelled, slowly walking around my car. "That b**** has gone too far. I can't believe this s***!"

Glen tried to calm me down. "Josh, just relax. Do you have insurance?"

"Yeah!" I said, staring at my car.

"Well, that eliminates half of the problem. Now that gal's the next thing. Let's get inside and call the police so we can get a report going."

As soon as I walked into the store I was being paged over the intercom. I picked up the phone and before I could say a word, I heard Amy's voice. "Drive your whore around in that, you Mother fu****."

"F*** you, You crazy bi***!" I slammed the phone down, still mumbling to myself.

"Stop, come sit down," said Glen. Motioning for me to follow him. I fell into one of his office chairs. "Try and calm down," he said, handing me a Coke.

"I can't believe she did this."

"Don't worry, Josh. You're a young man. Believe me, you have far more sh** to go through with women," Glen said, massaging his knee.

"What's wrong with your knee?"

"Nothing… Just an old football injury. I played in the pro's you know."

"Really, what happened?" I asked.

"I took a hit that twisted me good and my knee paid the price. Thank God that I finished college or else I'd be another sad football story."

I started making my calls, first calling the police and then the insurance company. Both came out and took pictures. It took hours before everything was done and my car was towed to a repair shop. Glen volunteered to take me out for a drink and drop me off at home. A stiff drink was exactly what I wanted. We went to a sports bar where all kinds of professional ball players hungout. I'd heard of the place before. Word was that on Wednesday nights you couldn't get inside the place because that's the day all the super star players liked to come in. We drove up to the valet stop where the line seemed to be ten cars long. The parking lot was filled to capacity. I saw Porches, Ferraris, and there was even a Rolls Royce sitting right up front.

All kinds of beautiful women were walking past our car, heading for the entrance. Most of them were scantly clad. Many looked as though they could have been models. Glen and I finally got to the front of the valet line after minutes of waiting.

"How are you tonight, Glen?" The valet asked.

We approached the door, working our way through a sea of women and men waiting in line just outside. The doorman made way for Glen and me. I felt almost giddy. The women inside looked even better than the ones standing outside. They had perfect hair, teeth and perfect bodies, thanks to plenty of cosmetic surgery. Everywhere I looked I saw revealing outfits designer handbags and shoes. Glen came in shaking hands with some of the guys he knew. I had no idea he was so popular. He must have made quite an impact when he played football. There were all kinds of professional athletes there. I saw many from professional football and basketball teams and there were even a couple of television sports personalities. This place had a boxing ring dance floor, big screen televisions, table top soccer games, leather couches, and even a half size basketball court. There were neon and strobe lights flashing through out. The place also had an upstairs. I saw a few groups of people going up there. It must have been a private lounge because there were bouncers guarding the stairway.

Glen and I sat at the main bar and ordered drinks. He introduced me to a couple of guys standing nearby, one of them I immediately recognized from television. "You follow sports much, Josh?" Glen asked.

"I do occasionally. My favorite sport is boxing, but once in a while I watch these guys," I said pointing to a few players around me. "Usually when they start winning games," I chuckled.

I took a long look around the bar at all the beautiful women. *This is Unbelievable!* All these incredible women just waiting for a chance to screw a ball player. They were all living a big pipedream. They really thought they had a chance at locking up one of these guys. It was a big game that none of them would actually ever win. I guess to them it was well worth it to take a chance because if they did somehow happen to beat the odds, they wouldn't have to worry about money ever again.

"I didn't know women like this existed," I said, talking to Glen.

"Yeah, they exist alright. But remember, no matter how beautiful the woman, there is a man somewhere who's sick of her sh**," One of Glens friends said, who was standing in front of us.

"I'd like to have that problem someday." I said, laughing lightly.

"Well Josh," Glen said, "Money may not buy love, but it sure as hell can buy you a sh** load of women."

• • • • •

After that experience, I felt as if it was definitely time for me to get my own place. I began my search using apartment guides. Money wasn't a problem for me anymore, so I looked for places that had fireplaces and views of the city. Since Gabrielle had a nice place of her own, I took her with me. I felt she could offer some good advice on things that I might overlooked without her.

I chose an apartment right outside of the city, a decent size place with a nice pool and gym. It also had a view of the city. I decided to have Gabby help me pick out furniture which was a big mistake. I had to make it clear to her that this was my place, not hers. She pointed out everything she liked, like a salmon-colored living room set. I wasn't sure what she was trying to do to me. I think she was deliberately trying to pick out furniture that would give the impression that a woman lived with me just incase I decided to sneak a woman over. I decided to postpone my furniture shopping until later in the week when I could go alone.

• • • • •

I stood in the middle of my brand new apartment grinning from ear to ear as the delivery men brought my new furniture through the door. Soon everything was unwrapped and placed in the right spot. My living room sofa was just the right shade of deep navy blue, with a bright multi-colored contemporary coffee table. The dining room set was off white with a granite base. My bedroom was done in black Lacquer, accented with a silvery marble finish. All I had to do now was buy pots and pans, dishes and silverware, sheets and towels.

I decided to call Gabrielle over so we could spend some time together and show her the furniture I picked. I was felling so good, I called and had her favorite restaurant deliver a little Italian food. I bought candles and fresh roses for the table vase to create a little ambience. It was twenty minutes to eight. I stuck the delivered dinners in the oven, figuring she would be arriving at any minute.

I was surprised to see gabby had brought a bottle of wine to christen my new place. She also had her overnight bag. We ate dinner by candlelight and chatted on the balcony as we enjoyed the beautiful view of the city. After dinner she slipped her apartment key into my hand.

Oh great. She wants to be apartment buddies. I wasn't going for it. I knew better than to trade keys. It's a ploy to check up on you when you least expect it. I gave her key back her. "Hang on to that, baby. Soon you will be turning it in to your apartment complex." She smiled big and put it back in her purse. I was getting better and better at thinking on my feet. Now she was under the illusion that I wanted her to move in someday. We finished off the bottle of wine while taking a bubble bath in my whirlpool tub; later breaking in the king-size bed .

· · · · ·

I was really enjoying my new position and the lifestyle change, but as weeks passed, some of the employees who secretly were jealous of my promotion started to show their true colors. Many of them refused to give me respect because of my age. I was almost twenty years younger than many of them. I decided they'd respect written warning's. I started writing-up anyone who was coming in late constantly or doing things they shouldn't be doing. After about five months, I got the respect I wanted. A few salesmen were let go during that time. I wanted to go to the convention in Las Vegas, so I needed great sales numbers from the store. Glen was till acting as temporary store manager, while training Earl to take the position. Glen needed to replace the salesmen that were fired, since the Christmas holiday was approaching. Because of sales numbers, I was put in charge of deciding who would be sent on to the second interview with Glen. We began looking for part-time sales people.

Glen wanted at least two pretty women hired. "Good-looking women bring in Business," he said. Applicants would come in at a rate of two to three a day. Some had experience, others had the drive. Some women did apply. I wanted single women only because, like most men, I wanted a shot at them. The guys were excited because, they knew I was dating a dancer and would hire some stunners if I could. I wanted to stay away from picking divorced women because I saw them as trouble. Who needs an agry woman in the store ready to scream sexual harrasment the minute you compliment her? Many men see a divorced woman as desperate, needy, and easy to get in bed.

If you ever wondered why it seems all the very attractive women get the good jobs, well now you know. In the world of men, we try to balance what the company needs and what we want when it comes to hiring women. We would never tell women that, but if you ever watch cable TV news channels, take a good look at the women on the program. They weren't hired for their talent to give the news, they were hired because some guy wanted a shot at having sex with them. He loved their beauty and good looks first; if they could do the job second. Don't forget, The world of men directly influences and controls the entire world. Somewhere there are incredible female news broadcasters with average looks, who will never get a shot because of it.

I was really into the screening of these potential hires, especially the females. I went as far as looking up their dates of birth in astrology books trying to get a clue as to which ones would be easiest to get into bed. We men do some crazy things when it comes to women.

A cute young girl right out of high school was one of the first females to apply. She was just too young. A couple of the guys were practically begging me to pass her through, but I wasn't going to throw her to the wolves. Many men Look for women much younger than them or foreign women, new to the country. They are the easiest to take advantage of because they haven't had much experience with men or this society. Remember we naturally think like predators, always looking for the weakest prey.

We men always have a plan, a plan for ourselves and one for the women in our lives. We always think ahead. Strategy comes naturally for us. It's something I've noticed while observing men and women in social enviroments. Men naturally, team up and women just "group up." A group doesn't have a chance against a team.

There was one applicant that caught my eye right away. Her name was Micheal Starn. I thought her name was really interesting. She was a multi-racial mystery, I guessed half Caucasian and half African-American with a touch of Hispanic. She wasn't married and had no sales experience but who cared? She had an awesome pair of legs and a stunning face. She worked as a model and carried herself like she was a super star. I loved the way she dressed for the interview, a see-through white blouse and a tight brown leather skirt which hugged her butt just right. As far as I was concerned, she had the job.

There was one other women who I liked. She was in her early thirties, sort of plain but very pleasant, not much make-up, and wore dated clothes. I didn't see a wedding ring so I assumed she wasn't married. I figured she may have been recently divorced. I probably wouldn't have sent her on the the second interview, but we had no other good applicants. Her name was Amanda Reed and during the interview, she constantly flirted with me. She spoke in a seductive tone and kept adjusting her bra. I knew it was all an act, obviously she had been around and knew just what it took to get noticed for a job. It was like she was auditioning for a movie or something. I called her the "mattress actress," though not to her face, of course.

After getting through all of the B.S. acting, it turned out she had a ton of sales experience. I recommended two gentleman for the positions. Combined, they didn't have the sales experience of Amanda, but they had enthusiam.

It was about a week later when I noticed that all four of my recommendations passed their interview with Glen. I didn't know which excited me more, having Micheal work with me or that Glen approved of my choices. The men at work loved having two new women on staff. Some were even placing bets on which one would they would get into bed first, reminded me of the girl betting at the college parties.

Yes, guy's often place bets with other men, on which women they will have sex with. Work became fun, it was nice having a couple of good-looking women around me, asking questions. I was always willing to help. Because I helped to get them hired, I think they treated me better than they normally would have.

Sometimes I'd be swamped with paperwork when one of them would volunteer to help me out. Once in a while I'd take them up on the offer because I was still new at being assistant manager and could always use some help.

Amanda and Micheal both had boyfriends. Amanda's boyfriend use to always arrive late to take her home. During Amanda's second month on the job she brought him in and introduced him to me. I could see in his eye's that he was a little intimidated.

After that brief meeting, he was never late and most of the time came early to pick her up. I loved it. There's nothing better to boost a man's ego, than to make another man feel insecure. It didn't help that Amanda was already a pretty good actress. I'm sure her boyfriend never knew what she was thinking. Women like that are fun, but dangerous for men. Even I wasn't sure if she liked me or not, but I enjoyed her company anyway. She always pretended to listen and she loved to give me her sexiest stares which sometimes threw my mind into man mode. I could just see myself taking her to the men's room, biting and kissing her, until she'd beg me for it.

Micheal was a different story. She flirted with me only when we were alone. She never talked about her boyfriend around me, but often did around the other employees. To me this was a big invitation. There wasn't a single day that passed that I didn't think about her in some way. Always a sucker for the exotic or different looking women, the temptation of Micheal was becoming unbearable.

Months passed and Gabrielle and I were still a couple. I hadn't given her my apartment key yet, but we were seeing a lot of each other. I'd see her on her days off or she'd come by my place after work. My work life grew more and more tempting each passing day. I was still being given the green light by Amanda, but so was Glen. She was definitely looking for someone either going somewhere, or someone who already was somewhere.

One evening in December, fate paid Micheal and me a visit. We were both working until close. Running late to work that morning, Micheal had inadvertently left her car lights on. Everyone else was gone for the night all except Micheal who had come back in after learning her car battery was dead.

"Josh, can I make a quick call home to see if Jason's home? I left my damn lights on and my battery is dead."

"Sure," I said. "Go right ahead."

Jason was Micheal's boyfriend and I was torn. Part of me wanted Jason to be home, and part of me didn't.

"Damn!" she said, slamming the telephone reciever down. "He's never around when I need him."

"Don't worry, Mike, I'll take you home."

"Really?"

"Oh course."

"Thank you, Josh, I owe you one... Really."

"You don't owe me anything. It will be my pleasure." I said, winking. "Hey, want to stop off and get something to eat on the way, I haven't eaten all day?"

"I guess so. I didn't have anything planned for tonight anyway."

"Good. Give me a few more minutes to finish up here."

I went to the office to finish up. Micheal took of her coat and pulled up a chair next to me. I could see she was a little pissed about her car battery, so I tried to get her mind off of it by complimenting her and planting some sexual seeds. "I must say, Micheal, your make-up and hair has been rocking the last couple of days. How do you do it?"

"Really? Nah, it's awful. I was thinking about getting it cut a little." She said, playing with a piece of her hair, looking at the ends.

"No, don't do that. Your hair is beautiful. Besides, what would I pull on, if you Were to cut it?" Still playing with her hair, Micheal stared at me. "Your so good looking," I said. "I bet if you were bald, you'd still look amazing," I said, flirting a little more. Micheal just smiled at me.

"What are you doing." she asked, rolling her chair closer to see.

"Wow, do you always smell this good?" I asked. Her smile got even bigger. "Do you mind? I'm trying to finish up here," I said playfully. "It's hard to concentrate when your sexy a** is almost in my lap."

Micheal laughed and said, "Keep the compliments coming and maybe it will be."

I could see where this night was headed. I finished up, set the store alarm system and we were off to dinner. I took her to one of my favorite spots, a little jazz club downtown. We took our seats at the bar.

"I've never been here before," she said. "It's so nice here."

"Yeah, it's one of my favorite places. They have great live music here. What are you drinking tonight?" I asked.

"Hum," she said, looking over the drink menu. "I think I want a dirty martini."

"Good choice, I'll have one too." We ordered finger foods and had light conversation. We flirted for another twenty minutes, then the conversation got really good as I knew it would. After all, she was drinking a martini. I like to call it the liquid panty remover. It's the one drink that always seemed to get me laid. Soon we both started to giggle a bit more and stare into each other's eyes when we spoke.

I knew I had her where I wanted her. "You know what Micheal? I like you... I like you a lot." She didn't say a word, just smiled. I sat back and watched Micheal as she turned and listened to the jazz band. She was so relaxed,. She just swayed her head and body to the slow, smooth rhythm. Of course, I was scouting the bar for other women while she wasn't paying attention. There were so many classy women enjoying themselves, all sizes, ages and races. On my way to the men's room, a thought occurred to me, *How is a man suppose to stay faithful with all this beauty in the world?* I returned to Micheal minutes later. I walked up behind her and whispered in hear ear. "Lets' get you home." My lips were so close to the back of her neck and ear lobe, I had to smell her and kiss her neck a little.

"Oooh, that tickled." she said, flinching a little. I could tell she loved it. I followed her as we started to my car. From behind her, I put my hands around her waist. We stopped steps from the car. I bent down and put my cheek next to hers, smelling her hair and feeling the back of her neck and ear with my lips and nose.

"Damn you feel good," I said closing my eyes to enjoy the feeling. I'm sure hers were too because she was enjoying it so much she laid her head back against my chest and started breathing a little heavier. I opened the passenger door for her and she slid in slowly. The martini had done it's job. She was very relaxed and playful. I got in and started the engine, while waiting for the car to warm up. Micheal took off her shoes and curled her legs upon the seat.

"Are you comfy?" I said, smiling.

"Oh yes," she said. Her eyelids were half open.

"Take off your coat, babe. It'll warm up soon."

I took off my coat and suit jacket. "Okay, which way do I go?" I asked.

"Take the freeway."

We were only on the freeway a few minutes when Micheal put her head next to mine. I pretended not to notice as she gave me a kiss on the ear. I didn't say a word. She did it again trying to provoke a reaction out of me, which she did.

"I'm trying to drive here," I said, smiling. I looked over to see her putting her hand down her shirt smiling at me. I was starting to get really aroused. She then started unbuttoning my shirt. "Baby, I'm trying to find an off ramp, hold on."

She reclined her seat and slowly started taking off her skirt and panties. *This is going to be good.* I immediately pulled to the shoulder of the highway and turned on the hazard lights. Ah, the rush of forbidden sex. It never gets old.

I dropped Micheal home about thirty minutes later. Gabrielle didn't get off work until two o'clock in the morning and was suppose to come by. I had plenty of time to take a shower and fool myself into believing I'd simply gone to work and driven straight home alone. There was no way of getting Micheal out of my mind after that night. She had something special and I wanted much more.

Chapter 5

THE LOVE BUG

Bitten by the love bug. I started to push gabrielle away. I started missing her calls on purpose, hang-out with my friends a bit more, and when she asked me, why I was acting so weird, I made up a lie. I accused her of cheating with a bartender at the club. I didn't care. I liked Gabrielle a lot, but Micheal had an intense hold on me.

About five weeks later Gabrielle and I were done. It was finally time to make Micheal my girl.

Micheal and I hadn't seen much of each other since our freeway experience. Things started to slow down after the holidays and her hours were cut back. I knew she would be coming in to work Thursday afternoon and I was ready for her. That Thursday we exchanged looks and smiles all afternoon. I was so happy to see her. I waited until two hours before closing to ask her out.

"Micheal, if you help me close up, will you take me out tonight?" I asked.

"Let me get this straight, you want me to help you close up and then take you out?" She said, with a confused expression. She thought about a few seconds. "You're crazy you know that?" We both giggled. We had an incredible chemistry with each other.

I left my car at work. Micheal recently had bought a new car and decided todrive. We couldn't stop smiling as we listened to the love ballad's playing on the radio. We went to a Greek restaurant just off the lake. We were seated in a dimly lit booth in the corner, it was very cozy and romantic. We placed our orders and the questions began.

"So, how are you and your boyfriend getting along?" I asked.

"What boyfriend, I got rid of him weeks ago."

Ooh! This was music to my ears. Either he had screwed up or our freeway escapade left a very pleasant memory for her.

"I heard you have a very pretty girlfriend. You two getting along?"

"No, I sure don't. I was kind of dating this one girl, but that's over now."

She smiled and sipped her drink. "That's too bad. She didn't know what she had."

"I guess not."

Micheal gave me a soft stare. I stared right back, playing with my own drink straw. "You are fascinating." I felt a chill flow through my body as I continued to stare. *I could really love this woman.* We were interrupted by our waiter bringing our lamb dinner's. Micheal was wonderful company, so beautiful and interesting. It was a wonderful connection I felt with her I'd never felt with any other woman. For the first time in my life, I was falling in love.

After dinner, I asked Micheal to spend the night with me. That way we could leave for work together in the morning. We stopped off at her house to get her clothes and make-up and then we went to my apartment where we stayed up almost all night talking. I felt like I had a new best friend and lover. Later that night we had some pretty passionate sex. The odd thing is I wanted to snuggle her afterwards. I knew I had to be in love.

Months passed and Micheal and I were really getting along well. We were doing a good job at keeping our relationship from the other employees, even though we took a lot of risk's. We'd sneak kisses whenever we thought no one was around. We'd go out to lunch and have sex in the parking lot and we were almost always together. It was great.

Glen had finally left the store for Earl to manage. I think earl knew about Micheal and me, but he wasn't the kind of guy who would say anything. I decided a short time later that Micheal and I should move in together. It was fun having her live with me. She loved the arts, dance, plays and writing, just like me.

· · · · ·

Just as I thought everything was going great, something happened. That powerful, male urge started to knock. I was doing so well. I ignored women when they gave me complements and bedroom eyes. I tried to not notice other women when I was out with Micheal. I was being as good as I could, but the urge was always there, waiting. I wasn't even bored with Micheal. Like so many men, we have a great relationship with the women we love and suddenly it's playtime. Some say a man begins to wonder if he still has it. Maybe he misses the thrill of the hunt. Other men say the constant teasing in our male social world plays a role. You see, we often ridicule men who are in committed relationships, causing the man to want to prove himself to their friends. I find it happens more with progressive, driven men. It's the old, "more is better" mind set.

Some women think it's their fault a man strays. Don't believe it. We can't stop the little voice, no matter how hard we try. I was a great example of this. I had a women who I loved and cared for, but my loyalty was beginning to weaken.

· · · · ·

Soon I was back to my old tricks. The first person that came to mind was Gabrielle. I hadn't completely gotten over her. I often wondered what it would be like to have both Micheal and Gabrielle at the same time. I knew Micheal definitely wouldn't go for it, but hey, that's how the male mind works, always trying to turn fantasy into reality.

• • • • •

On one of my off days, while Micheal was out on a modeling shoot, I snuck over to the topless bar where Gabrielle worked to see what I could make happen. I arrived around five o'clock in the afternoon. I ordered a drink and sat in the same booth where I'd sat the first time I saw her. I sat there for almost twenty minutes and there was no sign of her. I told myself, *Two more songs and I'm out of here.* I finally saw her walking out from the dressing room, looking better than ever.

She walked right by, staring straight ahead as she passed. "Gabby! Gabby!" I yelled her name three more times before she finally stopped.

"What do you want a**hole?" She said, with a angry expression.

"Please baby, can I have a word with you… please?" I tried my best to look humble.

She reluctantly walked back to the booth and sat down. "Say what you have to say, Josh, then go the f*** away."

"I understand you're mad, but please hear me out. I'm sorry… I'm so sorry. I don't know what was wrong with me." I paused and looked down shaking my head for effect. "I'm sorry I accused you. I know you wouldn't do that, but I guess this job you have plays games with my head. I'd like to make it up to you. Can I take you out shopping sometime? I want to make it up to you."

If looks could kill, I would have died instantly.

"F*** you, Josh! You are a complete piece of sh**. F*** you two times," She said, throwing up two fingers and getting loud. "You really think I'm stupid, huh?"

Gabrielle stood up, pointed at me, and gave me one last "F*** you!" before walking away.

"The hell with you! I didn't want your sorry ass anyway," I yelled, as she left. I couldn't believe her. She really tried to embarrass me.

I sat there for several minutes trying to calculate my next move, while I nursed my drink. "Excuse me," I said to a passing dancer. "Hi, I remember you from high school. Carrie, right?" I motioned for her to sit with me. I figured getting a few dances from her, would drive Gabrielle crazy. I ordered her a drink as we talked a little about high school. I got the feeling she didn't like me much. She was very dry and vague with me. I decided to move things along in case she was the all business type of dancer. "How about a couple dances and then maybe I could take you out sometime," I said.

"What?" she said as if she was turned off by the idea.

"I asked if you would like to spend some time with me. Something wrong with that? You're a good looking woman."

"No way," she said in a snippy tone.

"Have I done something to piss you off?" Her attitude confused me.

"For your information, I prefer women, not men. Thank god for that because if I was straight, I'd be just as screwed up as Gabrielle. I bet you haven't even noticed what you've done. I suppose your needs are more important to you than her feelings, huh?" She opened her handbag and applied another coat of lipstick.

"Listen, what goes on between Gabrielle and me is none of your damn business." I was starting to get a little pissed off.

"You men screw with these girls heads, you play your little games and lead them to believe they're special. After you get what you want, you throw them away and move on to someone younger and prettier. You men have absolutely no god damn feelings." Carrie got up and stormed away.

"The hell with all of you," I said, leaving the bar at a brisk pace.

I drove home thinking about all that happened. Carrie had a point. I was as wrong as a man could be. I started to think that maybe it was time to get serious and consider marriage. Some of the guys I'd talked to said marriage did kind of helped them stay out of trouble.

• • • • •

For the next couple of weeks I started to ask other men for advise on the idea. The great majority of men were against it. I got plenty of men saying, "don't do it, Josh. Wedlock is just that, locked." I was concerned about cheating when married. The common rule amongst men is that, it's not cheating if you haven't been caught. I also got some guys that felt that if I was going to do it, to make sure I stayed in control… meaning, keep them [women] under the illusion that they have control by simply telling them they were. A wealthy customer of mine named Anthony pointed out something I will never ever forget. His father was a politician and like his father, he was always ready to give advise. He said "You treat a marriage like the presidency. You're the president and your wife's the first lady. The president has power and the first lady has no power at all, but the illusion is that she does, because we have convinced women in to thinking she does." He said, "The first ladies was nothing more than house wives that we decided to give titles to. This is why we don't have to worry about a women president. Women believe, as long as there is a first lady, they have a voice. Always make your wife believe she has power and you will be fine."

What Anthony said really opened my eyes. How many times have we heard a man proudly say, *she's the boss*, when speaking with someone in the presence of their wife or girlfriend. I began to learn that deception, and misdirection are powerful tools of the code.

I knew I wanted to give marriage a try one day and felt Micheal and I could probably do well. I decided to go to a local jewelry store the next day, to see what I could find to show Micheal just how much I cared about her.

The next day I went to a local jeweler and I picked out a two karat diamond solitaire ring. I wanted to really let Micheal know I was serious about a future with her. I drove to a local florist and bought two dozen long-stemmed red roses and picked up a bottle of champagne on the way home. I was going to give Micheal an unforgettable night. I figured I'd pop the question the minute she got home. I placed on dozen roses on the dining room table and picked off all the petals from the rest and made a trail of flower petals leading from the front door to the bedroom. I placed her gift on her pillow. I heard the door open as scheduled. She was right on time.

"Oooh! What's going on, Josh? She yelled. "What are you trying to do?" She giggled. I could hear her following the path. "This is a surprise." she said, walking into the bedroom.

"Hi baby." I said. Sitting on the end of the bed.

"Are you trying to be romantic?" she said, with a big smile. "What is that?" she asked, pointing to the present on her pillow.

"Open it." I saw nothing but teeth, as she carefully opened the wrapping paper.

"No way! No way!" she repeated a couple more times, as she discovered her gift was a black ring box.

I took the ring from the box and got down on one knee. "Micheal, there's something I'd like to say. I'm in love with you and I want you in my life for as long as I live. Will you marry me?" She was actually shaking when I put the ring on her finger.

"Yes, Josh. Yes, I will," she said, starting to tear up. She gave me the most passionate kiss that I had ever had. I felt all of her love in it. We sat on the end of the bed holding each other. With tears in her eyes, she said, "Josh, I love you."

We kissed and hugged for another few minutes. It felt so good. I'd never made anyone so happy in all my life. It was an incredible feeling.

Micheal immediately started calling all her friends and relatives. It meant the world to her. I laid down on the bed enjoying her happiness. *Wow! I actually proposed!*

After Micheal finished making her calls, we decided to stay home and celebrate. We popped open our bottle of champagne and had steak and lobster dinners delivered from a local steak house. She couldn't stop looking at her ring. It was a beautiful night.

A few days later, everyone knew Micheal and I were engaged. Her ring was the biggest clue. I was getting negative reaction from a lot of men. They told me I was making a big mistake and that there was no way, I would be faithful for long. I knew it would happen. Men are secretly really against marriage. To most men, it's seen as the worst possible thing a man can do.

The jeering slowed after a few weeks. Everyone but Earl got the message. Every other day he'd start some trash talk and I was growing tired of it. One afternoon he started in on me. "So when's the big day," he asked.

"No date yet, Earl, One step at a time. How many times do I have to tell you?"

"Josh, you know damn well, you wont keep it in your pants. You just doing all this for fun?"

"Don't worry about it. Why are you so interested in what I'm doing?"

"Just looking out for you man," he replied.

"Do yourself a favor and look out for you." I said, getting a little angry.

"Okay, okay, I didn't know you were so sensitive." I think Earl had a crush on Micheal and was pissed off that I was taking her off the market.

• • • • •

Word began to circulate about a company buyout. An employee brought in a newspaper article which talked about our company having negotiations with a larger competitor. I had a feeling that the company would be sold. The electronics and computers business was constantly changing all the time anyway. It was time to think much bigger

Micheal and I enjoyed ourselves in the meantime. We did lot's of shopping and clubbing, even going on short trips and vacations together. All this fun created even more pressure on me to marry her. Her family was starting to wonder if I was actually going to marry her at all.

• • • • •

One night, Micheal's grandparents invited us over for dinner, for no particular reason. I really wasn't in the mood to go, but I knew it would mean a lot to Micheal. She loved her grandparents a great deal. They'd helped to raise her when she was a child. We arrived at her grandparents' house at seven o'clock. Both sides of the street were lined with cars. I entered the house and saw about twenty of her family members, brothers, uncles, aunts and cousins. I wasn't fooled for a minute. It was nothing more than a team of marriage supporters, ready to pressure me into marriage. I knew it was coming because I'd overhead some of Micheal's conversations with her relatives. I'd often hear her defending my slow pace towards the alter.

I went inside with my head held high, ready to do battle. Her relatives were all very nice until the end of dinner. From what Micheal had told me, her grandmother Marie, was a woman who spoke her mind. She was the catalyst. "Joshua, let me ask you a question. When are you going to marry my granddaughter?" She asked, as we sat at the dinning room table having dessert. I had my excuse's ready.

"We plan on getting married once we see what happens with work. Looks like a buy-out is imminent."

"That's all the more reason for you and Micheal to get married, It takes two people to make it nowadays," her grandfather Victor said, joining the conversation.

"Well, we plan on having a big wedding, and we can't do that if we're both unemployed. You all want to be there don't you?"

"No, we don't have to be there to see you get married," Marie said. "You two make such a beautiful couple, we just want the best for you."

"Nothing will make us happier Josh, than to know you and Micheal are legally married" Victor said.

"Well, sir." I said. That's all I could say before being interrupted by Victor..

"Son, listen to me. Micheal is my oldest granddaughter. I want to know she's married before I pass away." *Oh boy, He's laying it on thick.* Everyone seemed to be nodding in approval as I paused and glanced around the room. I was really being put on the spot.

"We'll see what happens, but I'm set on having a big wedding," I said.

"Why don't the two of you just get married at the courthouse?" It's cheap and you can be married in a couple of hours," one of Michaels's cousins blurted.

I was growing tired of thinking up comebacks, so I just let them talk until they Decided I'd heard enough. They continued for another thirty minutes. They probably would have kept going if I didn't decide to pack it in and go home. It felt so good to get in the car and away from their onslaught.

"I'm sorry baby," Micheal said, starting the car.

"Don't worry about it. I knew it was going to happen. I didn't realize it was so important to them."

"They just want to make an honest women out of me," she said with a big grin. We drove home talking and chuckling about it all.

• • • • •

A week later during our weekly store meeting, Earl announced that the company was going to be sold, Everyone was talking about leaving and finding work at other electronics' stores. Micheal and I had already begun looking long before the announcement. I decided to look into the job market in Las Vegas after seeing on television that they planned on building several new hotel casinos over the next few years. I searched online, gathering more information on housing and cost of living for the city. Las Vegas was in need of professional people to fill the up coming positions in the gaming industry. I knew this was the right move to make. I sprang the news to Micheal when she came home.

"Baby, I have some good news. I've found the solution to our job problem."

"Okay, continue," she said.

"Las Vegas. We should move to Las Vegas," I said, excitedly. I showed her the pages of information I printed out from the computer. "As you can see here, the job market is starting to grow and the cost of living is actually less expensive then here."

She took the pages from my hand and sat down on the sofa. She looked it over once and said. "I'm not going."

"Why not?" I said, puzzled.

"I'm not going to some god forsaken town, where I don't know anyone. What if something were to happen to you? Tell you what, the only way I would consider going is if we were married." She walked into the kitchen and poured herself some juice.

"So your giving me an ultimatium?" No man wants to be forced into marriage, but I have to give her credit, she was smart. I would have done the same thing if I were in her position. "Marriage is just a piece of paper," I said. Trying to convince her to see things my way.

"How can you say such a thing? Marriage is a commitment between two people in the sight of God." she said, becoming very serious.

We continued our discussion for hours. I gave up eventually. I decided to take a bath to sit and think. Micheal had made a valid argument and

I did love her. I knew one day that I'd marry her. While in the bath tub thinking, I decided I would go ahead and surprise her on Valentines Day with an elopment.

Later that week I called the courthouse downtown to found out what was needed to get a married. I took Micheal out for a little shopping and told her to pick out a beautiful suit for valentines day because I was going to take her to a very special place.

• • • • •

Valentine's Day morning I was all set to go. The courthouse would need both of our birth certificates so I put Micheal's and my birth certificate in my suit jacket pocket. I thought I'd have cold feet, but I didn't. The morning was just like many others we had together. We fought over the bathroom and made jokes about each other just like we'd done many morning before. When I stopped to think about it, possibly spending the rest of my life with her wouldn't be so bad. We got into the car and started driving towards downtown. "I know what you're doing." she said.

"What?" I knew she didn't have a clue, but I was interested in hearing what she thought.

"Your taking me to some fancy brunch." she said, nodding like she'd guessed right.

"Oh babe, before we get to the big surprise, I need to stop off and pay these parking tickets. Do you mind, it'll only take a few minutes?"

"Okay, just make it fast, I want to get to this big secret of yours." She was totally Fooled and I loved it.

We walked up to the courthouse together. Once we entered the building a security guard directed us on which way to go. I guess because it was Valentine's Day and the way we were dressed clued him in. Micheal mentioned that she had money with her if I didn't have enough to cover the tickets. I just smiled and thanked her. She was so cute. We found the room after a short walk. Inside, it looked like a elementary school classroom. There were red paper hearts hanging all over the windows and a big oak desk. The room was small, but had a cathedral ceiling.

"Good morning, you're our first couple today. I'd think there would be a line out the door since it's Valentines Day," she said with a happy smile. She then asked for both our birth certificates and drivers licenses.

"What's going on?" Micheal asked. It was starting to sink in.

"You said you wouldn't go to Vegas with me unless we got married, so were getting married," I said, holding her hands and shaking them a little. Micheal was speechless. For a moment, I thought she was going to back out on me. She seemed dazed. After we'd finished signing all the paper work we were told to go down the hall and make a left where a Justice of the Peace was waiting to marry us. Once we left the room, my bride came back to life.

"I can't believe you did this to me," she said shaking her head as we walked down the hall.

"Your not mad, are you?" I asked.

"No, I just can't believe you." When we got to the stairs we met Justice of the Peace Harriet snow. We shook her hand and introduced ourselves, handing her our paperwork.

"Let's get started," she said.

Micheal cut her short. "Right here, on the stairs? Don't we get a room?" Snow just shook her head. I gave her the go ahead and the ceremony began. In a matter of minutes we were married. To be honest, I didn't feel any different and I'm sure Micheal didn't either. I stopped off to buy flowers and chocolates and then we had brunch at one of the best restaurants in the city. When we got home I painted a picture for Micheal as my personal wedding gift to her.

Later that evening we started planning for the big move to Las Vegas. She couldn't believe we were actually going to leave. We planned on leaving in one week. We had a lot to do. We had to find an apartment near Las Vegas, employ a moving company, arrange for hookup of utilities, ship our cars, and so forth. The week couldn't end fast enough.

We both had a serious case of the butterflies as the final day was upon us. A few family members and friends came over to see us off. That was one of the saddest days of my life. I think everyone but the movers had tears in their eyes. We said our goodbyes and off we went to the airport.

We were both well prepared for this big change, but nothing could have prepared me for what was to come. I would soon see, that the secret world of men was far darker and deeper than I ever imagined.

Chapter 6

ASIAN PERSUASION

We arrived at McCarran International airport at ten o'clock in the morning. Micheal and I were filled with excitement and enthusiasm. I could see that she was very nervous. We walked out of the airport and found a taxi. The taxi line reached all the way around the airport terminal. Micheal loved the sunshine and the palm trees swaying in the wind.

We pulled up to our new home about thirty minutes later. I could tell that I was going to like it here as soon as we got out of the taxi and walked past the pool to the clubhouse. My eyes were all over the place. There were women out sunbathing nearly naked. I said to myself, *This is the place for me*. I looked out of the corner of my eye, only to see Micheal looking out the corner of hers at me. She knew I was looking, but how could I not? Some of those girls had beautiful tanned skin, not to mention perfect breast.

Shortly after we signed our paper work we were shown our new apartment. It wasn't too bad. We had a partial view of the clubhouse pool. Micheal thought it was a little small. I had to agree. It was a little tight and had almost no closet space. There wasn't even a hall closet.

We caught a taxi to a local car rental place. We went to the bank, got something to eat, then went sightseeing. We gambled a little and then went home to have our first night of sleep in our new place.

Our furniture and cars arrived two days later. After moving everything around and getting situated, it was time to find jobs. I went straight to Dealers school to learn blackjack. It was a very good school. The instructors were very knowledgeable. The ladies learning how to deal weren't too bad either. It wasn't always easy to pay attention. I found myself watching the students who would often come to class wearing next to nothing, because of the sunny Las Vegas weather.

Micheal found a job right away as a cocktail waitress. She didn't care much for the job, but at least we were paying bills from her paycheck and not our savings. I soon graduated from Dealer school and luckily got hired at a new casino right on the Las Vegas Strip.

It was fun mingling with people from all over the country. We had a great many guests from Arizona and California on the weekends and a general mix during the week. One of the things I liked most about working in the hotel casino industry was the conversations with men from all over the world. I found it interesting that men could be from totally different backgrounds, yet still protect the male code. It was as if we were all pre-programmed with it naturally. I also noticed that the majority of men were far more abrasive with their views regarding women, which was a little surprising to me.

I was now working with many men older than me who held very good jobs. Naturally they felt entitled and deserved respect, especially from the female employees. A great example was Jason Roc, a thirty-something Assistant casino manager who at first glance would strike you as a true professional. He was well-educated and well-traveled. Bleached blond hair, well-spoken and very charming, Jason appeared to be a perfect gentleman to all he met. He even had me convinced he was a pretty good guy until I got to know him better.

I was being trained to become a casino supervisor after only six months as a dealer because I learned all of the harder games and demonstrated professional conduct at all times according to my superiors. Actually I was just part of their little male brotherhood. Soon I'd be reporting and working with Jason directly.

Jason wasn't one to show his true colors until he felt he could trust you. Later I'd find out why. I learned that Jason had a very pretty girlfriend of more than seven years. They had a baby girl together. He had a couple of investment properties and a small business he was building outside of work. He made well over six figures a year, so he felt like he could do whatever he wanted when it came to the women in his life.

After months of working with Jason, he and I started having good conversations, often about investing, stock trading, and politics. Our conversations sometimes took a back seat to any pretty woman who would walk by. Jason and I were both into women, but for very different reasons. I'm a man who loves everything about women and find it hard to resist them. Like so many men I've met over the years, Jason seemed to want to dominate them and take away their self-respect. Jason, and men like him. Serve as a constant reminder that misogyny still flourishes in America.

Valentine's Day was coming up and I've always been a big fan of the occasion. That's why I chose to get married on that day. To many men totally dismiss Valentine's Day and other Sentimental days. I can't tell you how many times I've heard, "it's just another day" or it's a big commercial money pit." Who cares whether it is or isn't, I think it's fun to make the women of my life feel special.

I find it amazing that many men can get away with not giving or showing appreciation on such an important day, somehow convincing the women in their lives to pretend not to care about it either. Jason was a master of this kind of manipulation.

It was a week before valentine's day and I opened our conversation. "Jason, what are you planning for Valentine's day?"

"You're serious?" he replied after a short pause.

"Yeah."

"She's lucky to have me. I haven't given her anything in years. She doesn't need anything anyway."

"Women love getting stuff, you know."

"Yeah, a bunch of flowers they'll just throw away later," he said. "It's a waste of money."

I fully expected this attitude from Jason. He felt women were beneath him anyway. A very selfish man to begin with, like so many men in relationships, he used occasions like Valentine's Day to control the woman in his life. He had a daughter with his girlfriend, but refused to marry her. I played my games too, but I always believed that if you share a child with a woman you should step up. He just strung her along. Jason was also trying to have sex with every girl he could. Turns out he was involved with a cocktail waitress on another shift who was the girlfriend of a floor supervisor we worked with. His newest target was a cute little dealer who had just gotten hired a week ago. She was from the Philippines and he charmed her every chance he got. Poor girl had no idea what she was dealing with. "I'm going to destroy that little a**," he said, smiling and looking at her from across the casino floor.

"She is a cute little thing," I replied, looking in the same direction. "I heard she has an eight-year-old daughter."

"Oh yeah?" he paused for a few seconds.

"Yep."

"Guess I'll keep her around long enough 'til I can get two for one," he said with a serious look. I just stood there stunned. I couldn't believe what I'd heard. This guy not only wanted to take advantage of this new lady, but was also planning on her daughter too. Sometimes the thoughts of men can surprise and even shock other men. Unfortunately these monsters are able to exist because our male code hides them from view.

• • • • •

After that conversation I decided to keep my distance from Jason. He did open my eyes to just how selfish, sadistic and sick some men secretly are. I often wondered how all this disrespect came to be. Why does it continue decade after decade? Are women somehow perpetuating this type of behavior by not demanding the respect to which they're entitled? Why don't women just vote female candidates into office to gain respect for women in general? It amazes me to this day that women are the gender majority on the planet, but control absolutely nothing. Election after election casting their ballot for a man who of course is only going to look out for other men. He's part of the male code. Women have had the right to vote for other women for more than ninety years. A fifty-fifty gender balance in Congress is all it would take to not only balance America, but create more respect for women as a whole. The truth is men will not respect women until we see more of them in leadership positions.

• • • • •

I started making many friends, both male and female. Jackie was one of my favorite female friends. She's a young woman who loved to flirt with me and boy could she talk. Short black hair and a beautiful face. She would have been very much my type if she weren't so damn thin. This girl was super-skinny, but her personality made up for it. She was one of the most popular waitresses there. She was about thirty years old with two children from two different marriages. She and I were both big flirts. We had many good conversations, but there was one we had which stood out from all others.

Jackie dropped into work on her day off all dressed up to meet up with a couple of her waitress girlfriends. They were headed out to a nightclub. She decided to stop by the casino pit to say hello and show off, I suppose.

"Hey baby," she said with a wink.

"Hello," I replied, turning towards her, acting as if I didn't know who she was. I'd actually seen her come in several minutes before she got to me.

"Can I help you, miss?" I said with a smile.

"I'm sure you can," she said in a sexy voice.

"What you doing here, doll?"

"Boy, I'm here picking up my bi**hes. We're going to shake our a**es tonight."

"Oh," I said nodding.

I don't know how all this "it's-cool-to-be-a-bi***" stuff started. I understand it may be cool and fun, but understand it cheapens a woman in the eyes of men. We hear it and think it's okay to think of women that way.

"How do I look?" she asked, striking a pose like a ametuer model. "Do I turn you on?" She asked in a soft seductive voice. She was wearing all white clothes, white high-heel boots, a tight white dress, and a semi-transparent white blouse. Her hair and make-up were perfect.

"You're a beautiful lady."

"Lady?" she said, copping an attitude.

"Umm, yeah," I replied. I was a little taken aback by her snippy tone.

"I'm a girl, not a lady."

"Okay, you can be whatever you want," I said, trying to clam her down.

"Do I look old or something?"

"No babe, you look good. You look like a sexy young lady. Do you want to look like a girl?"

"Of course," she replied.

"Why?" I asked.

"because girls aren't old, that's why."

"babe, a lady gets respect, girls don't. You really don't want to be a girl."

"Whatever," she said, throwing up her hand as she strolled away. I began to think about what had just happened. It puzzled me why a thirty year-old woman would want to be a girl. Her daughter is the girl, not her. Like so many women out there, she was so very afraid of getting older. This was probably also why she couldn't keep a man in her life. Men like me don't want girls, we want a lady a partner. Girls are the women we cheat with and never call back. All she was doing in her delusional state of mind was attracting the worst types of men, the type that prey on a woman's insecurities.

Women don't know this, but we men can feel out a woman's weaknesses, taking whatever flaws a woman thinks she has and use them against her to control her. I call it the "predator's sense." We men can tell if a woman is divorced, gay, shy, smart, flighty, broken, depressed, needy, selfish, self-delusional, or desperate in just a few moments of observation. This is probably the first you have ever heard of this and you probably wont ever again. It's one of our biggest secrets.

Jackie is a prime example of someone who will constantly fall victim to this. She's been conditioned to believe that to be seen as a young lady was negative, but to be a party girl was a good thing.

• • • • •

Every Halloween in Vegas there was an annual event which was the epitome of this kind of male mind game. It was called the "Pimp and Ho" or "Players Ball" party. Mike and Sang would get very excited when these parties came to town. Mike was one of those hard-working super-social casino hosts who rubbed shoulders with all the top bosses in the casino and the hotel. They liked him because he'd organize many casino events like the Baccarat and poker tournaments. He was a big guy with a bald head. He'd played college football so he was a huge sports fan. I always thought he'd make a great sports agent if he ever changed professions. He knew many professional sports players in football and basketball and would fly them in for special events. He regularly played golf with the big brass. Like most men, he knew that golf was the way to open doors in your career. Mike had two children and a wife, which he rarely talked about. He could always be found schmoozing with the high limit players, high-end lawyers, Beverly Hills doctors…he knew them all. Heads of major companies, he knew them too. He was the guy you spoke to for those hard to get playoff tickets or if you wanted a good stock tip. Mike was all about progress in both business and his personal life. "Seven more years," Mike liked to say. He was counting down the years until he could leave his wife. He based it on his children's ages, the youngest being eleven at that time. He'd say once the last one hit eighteen he was going straight to his lawyer friend, get a divorce and disappear.

"Just seven more years, Josh," he said, walking behind me. "How many you have?"

"You know I don't have and kids yet."

"Then you have eighteen years," he said, chuckling. "Get that parachute fund together while your young, Josh. You're going to need it." Mike often spoke of a parachute fund which was supposed to be a secret bank account everyman should have that your wife was never to know about. I wondered how much mike had in his because he was always hanging out with his high-powered friends at the best strip clubs in town. Those girls don't come cheap. "I got some players flying in for the weekend to check out the Pimp and Ho," he said.

"Cool, I'll be here, I can't wait."

"What pit will you be in?" Mike asked.

"Ten, I'll be working with Sang."

"Got to love Sang," Mike said.

"Who you have coming in?"

Mike rattled off about eight names, all well known sports players.

"Very cool."

"I'll drop by the pit tomorrow and introduce you. Most of them have never experienced the magic of the Pimp and Ho," he said with a touch of street slang. He loved to impress everyone with his sports connections. I didn't mind. Everyone has their thing and sports was his. "Ah, Young T. and A. everywhere," he said with a smile.

"Yes sir," I replied.

"Talk to you later," Mike said, leaving the casino pit, checking his cell phone.

• • • • •

The following night I arrived to supervise my casino pit section. The always colorful Mr. Sang was already there ready to go. He'd be my casino pit boss for the night. Sang was a super-spirited Korean immigrant who had his priorities in order, or so it seemed. He and his hard-working wife and he lived very well: nice home, drove new cars, and their kids excelled in school and were being professionally trained in piano. He worked as a casino pit manager, usually in the high limit salon. His wife worked in the casino's Asian marketing department. Together they made a very good income. They seemed to have the American dream, but there's a reason it's called a "dream." In reality, Sang was an extremely sleazy sex addict.

Massage parlors that gave happy endings were his home away from home. This friendly, always cheerful, seemingly great guy was also the same guy who would show some of the most degrading pornographic pictures of women on his cell phone to all the guys when it was slow on the casino floor. Bondage, triple X and even bestiality excited him to no end. I always wondered what kind of men looked at that kind of stuff. When I met Sang I got my answer. Like I said before, the male world never ceases to shock and amaze me. Sang's big event of the year was actually a convention called Comdex, which took place about a month after the Pimp and Ho party. Comdex was a computer electronics expo, but also had a huge pornography section. Funny how a convention full of socially awkward computer geeks happens to occur at the exact same time and place as a pornography convention. Sang would always get free passes to

Comdex to meet his favorite porn stars. Sometimes he'd get invitations to these porno producer's private parties where they'd sometimes be filming movies while in Vegas. "I witnessed a live threesome," Sang would report later. " It was amazing, Josh."

I was always a little turned off by his adventures. Sure, I'm part of the male code like any other man, but the thought of a poor girl who somehow got mixed up with a bunch of complete animals and becoming a slave in their world of sadistic hardcore sex has always disturbed me.

Men like Sang (and believe me he's far from alone), they love to see women in these desperate situations. Sang is the reason why in some casinos the cocktail waitresses' break room has numerical code to get in. Someone knows how to keep those hidden predators away from their prey. This guy had a great life, two kids and a smart, well-educated wife to boot. If only his wife knew the real Sang.

"Hey Sang," I said, walking towards him as he was putting down the casino phone. "Ready for some serious eye candy tonight?"

"Hell! It's already started," he said pointing at the main casino path. I paused to look around the casino. It was early, but already we'd started to see guys in flashy pimp style attire, bright colored clothes, big hats and sunglasses. A few small groups of girls in half-naked 'ho' style clothes. Glass heels and corsets seemed to be the in thing. "It's Going to be a nice night," he said answering the ringing casino telephone.

• • • • •

A couple hours passed and so far all I was doing was standing around getting paid to watch half naked women. *Man, I love this job.*

"Hey Josh!" I turned to see Sang motioning for me to come to him. I walked over to see Sang staring at a girl wearing a dress that was simply incredible. It was made completely out of police crime tape.

"Wow! She's just begging for it." Sang said as I stood next to him.

Men immediately think that any time a woman is dressed scantly that they're whores. I know women love attention, but just be aware that you will almost always draw the worst kind of attention if you're improperly dressed. No woman wants to draw the attention of men like Sang.

"A dress made entirely of police tape," I said, staring. "That girl's got some guts."

She didn't have the best body, but with a strip of tape across her breast and maybe three strips across her butt, she was stopping traffic. It was just a matter of time before security was going to see her and ask her to cover up, so I tried to spend as much time looking as I could.

"She can't be wearing any panties so that thing is just out there," Sang said, smiling.

"Man oh man, they get better every year," a passing dealer said.

"I wouldn't mind getting a little of that," Sang said.

"Who wouldn't?" I said with a chuckle.

There were other reveling outfits as well. Another girl who stood out was wearing a large T-shirt as a dress. The shirt was so thin it was almost see-through with tears in all the right places. The back of the shirt was cut open all the way down to the crack of her butt. She completed the look with tattooed Japanese words running straight down her exposed back. Most of the women wore skirts so short that their butt cheeks would show every few steps because the skirts would rise as they walked. It was like a dream, all these young girls trying to upstage each other. It was times like this that made me wonder what had happened to women's push for equality. How in the hell did these guys convince their dates to wear this stuff out in public? I suppose it's the same magic spell that some how convinced women that working out with stripper poles was a good idea. Many of these girls were college students from different parts of the country. You'd think they'd be the last women on the planet to put themselves out like that. I noticed a few young ladies sitting down at one of the Blackjack tables in my section. I decided to walk over to get a better look.

"Hi, ladies, you all look stunning tonight," I said as charming as I could. They all smiled. One thanked me. One of the ladies reaching beneath the table, struggling to pull her skirt down.

"Baby, you knew it was short when you bought it," I said laughing a little. Her two friends laughed.

"There's enough wool in here to open a sweater store," Sang said from behind me.

"Get out of here," I said, motioning with my hand. "You trying to mess me up?"

"I get the two on the left," he whispered..

"Bye Sang."

"Okay, okay," he said, walking away. The ladies pretended not to hear him. In a brief man thought I envisioned myself having one of the chairs pulled back from the blackjack table and me slowly kissing her neck and slowly unbuttoning her blouse with one hand while running my fingers through her hair with the other.

"What's your name?" The question snapped me out of the fantasy.

"Josh, and yours?"

"I'm Maria and this is Nikki and Michelle."

"Nice to meet you," I said, nodding to them all. They all put their cash on the table and waited to play. Maria was the sexiest so I decided to flirt with her a bit. "You have the prettiest eyes," I said while the dealer was shuffling.

"Thank you. So do you."

"And a smile to match," I said quickly. Always attracted to exotic-looking women, Maria was definitely my type. She had a golden brown skin color with a sexy Spanish accent. "I love your accent. Where are you from?"

"Los Angeles."

"I love L.A.," I replied. "How did you get so sexy?"

"My mother's from Mexico and my dad is black," she said, smiling.

"That's a nice combination." We continued to flirt for a few more minutes.

"Cocktails! Cocktails!" a waitress announced walking past the table.

"How about a kiss on the neck,?" I asked Maria, staring at her. She wasn't sure what I meant and that's exactly what I wanted. I knew I'd thrown her for a loop with that one. "Isn't that a drink?"

"You're good," Maria replied. I just smiled. I knew I was getting to her because she became a little shy. They ordered their drinks and continued to play. I decided to back off and come back after they'd had a chance to loosen up with a little alcohol. I'd already warmed her up, now I just had to give her time. Once she got her drink in her, I'd go back and play some more.

About twenty minutes later I started to hear some giggling. That was my cue. I approached the table, standing about two feet away from Maria's side. I made eye contact with her in between her Blackjack hand signals. "Give me a big one," she said in a slow teasing manner, staring at the dealer and then at me.

"What are you going to do if you get a big one?"

"You'd be surprised," she replied with a wink. I knew the drink had put her right where I wanted her, so I pushed a little more to see what would happen. On one Blackjack hand she pretended to be having a little orgasm as she high-fived her friends.

"Wow! Did your toes curl too?" I asked.

"She wishes," Nikki said, chiming in.

"She wishes?" I said curiously. "You trying to tell me she never had one?" I asked. Maria just looked at me.

"That's amazing!"

"Guys don't care about that," Nikki said frowning.

I smiled. "Well this guy does." Maria perked up a bit. She was all ears now. "Nothing's better than taking care of your girl first in my opinion." I had the attention of all three now. "Making a woman climax is one of the best feeling in the world. I just love making their bodies tense up, then turning to jelly."

"Can I have your number?" Michelle asked, laughing. The others joined in. "That makes you one in a million."

"Guys I've met just want to get theirs and that's it," Nikki said.

"Unbelievable," I said, looking at Maria. I guess that's the difference between guys and men. It's about a complete experience in my opinion. See, I know once I take care of you, you'll be more than willing to give me anything I want, right?" I was looking in Maria's eyes the entire time.

"Stop Josh, you're making me hot," Nikki said, laughing. I later got Maria's number, but never called. I must have held on to it for over a week before finally throwing it away. Sometimes its just fun to have a little catch and release. A guys got to test his lures out from time to time.

After that night I thought, *No wonder I've done so well with women. Guys out here aren't even taking care of the ladies, just themselves.*

• • • • •

After a few years Micheal and I realized we had a pretty good life. We now owned our first home, a couple of very nice luxury cars, and had a nice savings account as well. Soon we were welcoming our daughter, Sterling, into the world. We were both trying to adjust to this big change. I did it by changing shifts, going from afternoons to day shift and later even trying the graveyard shift so someone would always be home with Sterling. In doing so I met just about everyone who worked there. I'd go out with co-workers from time to time and started to notice something about the men, they were all really into Asian women.

At times it seemed like most of the men in Vegas were. Sure, I'd see American guests with Asian women and think nothing of it, but after changing shifts and hanging out I realized it was a bigger deal than I had thought. Of course I can see why, some of them are very exotic and I'd always heard they are very attentive to their man. I have never been one to care what the race a woman was as long as they were sexy and had a nice body. I love women no matter what race, so it surprised me a bit when speaking with men that so many only wanted an Asian woman.

There was a security guard on day shift who was learning Chinese just to get a shot at a Chinese girl. *Who the hell does that?* I wondered. Like so many men who exclusively chase Asian women, he was far from attractive, socially awkward, and not at all manly, He was an average guy in every way, the kind of guy who didn't belong to any men's cliques. He'd make his rounds past the table games waiting for the Asian dealers' tables to go empty and then he'd make his move. I'd be watching the entire time. He'd open up with a few words of Chinese, smiling like he'd won the lottery. Soon after getting his accent corrected by the woman he was working on, the next thing you'd hear was "Maybe you can help teach me?"

I guess when you have no money and no game a man has to learn a foreign language to get laid. I've seen this time and time again in Vegas with the residents and visitors. All these beautiful woman visiting Vegas everyday and these men are only interested in a certain race of women? Something was wrong. I figured they were your weaker men so they went after what they considered to be the easier prey.

On the day shift I worked with a floor supervisor who shed some light on this. He called it the "yellow fever" and admitted to having it himself. James was a big guy, about six-foot-two, three hundred and fifty pounds easy, extremely overweight. He was a bit shy, probably because of his weight. Like sang, he loved massage parlors.

He'd ask me to go along with him from time to time. He was all about the happy endings. I always declined. Anytime I'd get bored of Micheal, I'd just watch one of my adult movies. A man has to have some porn to keep us out of trouble. James often bragged about how much money he saved because of his so-called Asian concubine, a Chinese girl he lived with. He was your typical male opportunist. The poor girl had a daughter and probably felt her options were severely limited. Being new to the United States, She'd probably been looking for some companionship, only to end up being used by this lousy, overweight loser year after year.

James said Asian women were better than American women because they did nothing but work and they were easier to control. "Asian women don't give you a hard time. They're easy to train." I'd just look at him and shake my head. This complete loser really thought he was something. The truth is no other woman would ever give him a chance, so he preys on the naïve. Sure I'd played my games with women, but never have I used them to get ahead. A real man makes his own way.

He doesn't take a woman's money or use her. What's sad is I met many Asian woman who didn't seem to mind being poorly treated by men. James would tell you it's part of their culture and that they were made to serve men.

• • • • •

I made friends with Lisa a co-worker from Thailand. She was raised in California and she's very attractive. She's very smart and a little on the crafty side, but we had good conversations. She had a thing for tall Caucasian American men. I would answer questions she had about men and relationships. Lisa loved to gamble, which usually put her into trouble every month. Even though she got support from her sister who was her roommate, she owed money to almost every guy she knew except for me. I wasn't as foolish as most men. She'd get close to men and whenever she ran out of money, she'd offer herself in exchange for cash. At this point I'd seen the game before, so I decided that casual friends is all we'd ever be. I remember going out for drinks with her once. She wanted to talk about her relationship with this guy who was a Motocross rider. She had a huge crush on him and he was actually playing her, doing the old "breakup to makeup" on her. The guy was just toying with her. We met at one of the Strip's smaller casinos after work.

"So what's happening, doll?" I asked, pulling out a chair to sit down. She was already sitting down, playing with her cell phone.

"Hey Josh," she said, glancing up for a moment. "I ordered your favorite, an extra dirty martini and Calamari."

"Thank you," I said, looking around the restaurant. "How is Julian?" Julian was her fourteen-year-old son who stayed with his grandfather in Los Angeles.

"He's staying out of trouble, so…" she said nodding.

"Good."

"Oh, Josh. I gotta tell you about Rich."

"What? He finally decided to make you his girl?" Rich was the Motocross guy she couldn't get enough of.

"Not officially, but he took me out last Saturday and we had so much fun. He bought me a cheerleader outfit to wear."

"What?" I said with a puzzled look. "You went out dressed like a cheerleader?"

"Yes… And we had so much fun," she repeated, smiling.

"Babe, your like thirty-three right? Why would you let him put you in that?"

"It was just a fun thing to do, Josh."

"I understand that and maybe if you were his wife or you two had been a couple for a while it would be okay, but it sounds like this guy may have a problem. You need to be checking his computer for child porn."

"It's not that serious, josh."

"Lisa, any man who asks a thirty-three year old woman to dress like a sixteen-year-old cheerleader has got something wrong with him. Look, you're a very young-looking woman. You're short and your body isn't much bigger than a preteen's. This guy sounds like he may be into kids. I'm not joking. There are some very sick men in the world. Your not a guy so you don't know"

"Nah, Rich isn't like that," she said, shaking her head.

"Tell you what, if that loser tells you to call him 'Daddy' when your having sex, get up and run," I said, trying to soften the mood. "This guy isn't right, Lisa. I know you wish he was, but he's got some serious red flags. Trust me on this one."

Lisa listened, but I knew nothing was going to sink in. She was a player and maybe it was her time to finally get played. We ate a little and finished our drinks. Later at her house I met her sister. Her sister's boyfriend was staying there with them. He was about twenty-five years older than her sister. This is something you see a lot in Vegas, young Asian women with much older American men.

After some small talk inside we went out on the patio where Lisa tried to put a little move on me. "Josh, I'm surprised Micheal let you come out with me."

"Let?" I said, chuckling. "She doesn't own me and I don't own her. We both try to be honest with each other. She's my girl. It's all about honesty." Lisa gave me a funny look while intentionally brushing her bare leg against mine.

"Would you like a massage?" she asked, trying to look into my eyes. I looked at her and laughed a little. "My bedroom is right there," she said, pointing to a window on the second floor on the back side of her house. I stood up, looked her straight in the eye and said, "It's not gonna happen, babe."

While driving home I thought, *Man, I can't believe she tried to bait me. I didn't mind the approach. Hell, if she had a little more body on her I would've been in serious trouble.* I liked going out with different women from time to time. I enjoy all the different conversations with women. Most guys like the company of men, but I've always prefer the company of women. Micheal never really gave me a problem when I'd go out. We made a promise to always be honest with each other. I think she understood me because there was nothing we didn't talk about.

I often wonder if good relationships go bad because of the lack of honesty. Men need to have contact with other women. Of course the temptation to bed our female friends will always be there, but that's what makes life exciting.

That situation with Lisa reminded me of something that some of my co-workers did twice a year. They'd save up their money for trips to Thailand and come back talking about their dirty adventures. They'd go on and on about how you can buy young girls cheap and how they will do anything you ask. Vietnam and the Philippines were also destinations they visited. I knew these guys were just going to these countries to exploit poor, desperate young women. I mean what makes grown men travel halfway around the world to third world countries to have sex with impoverished young girls? Just another dark, disgusting side of our secret world. What makes it worse is that these America men would sometimes be escorted by men originally from these Asian countries. I know and live in the male social world like the next man, but to treat the women of your native country like common whores was just mind boggling. Just goes to show you that the Male Code is even stronger than the love for women of one's homeland.

• • • • •

The Las Vegas Strip was in need of talented professionals for its luxury hotel casinos. A couple of very high-end hotel casinos were about to open. I was pretty much told to be ready to move on by some of the top bosses at my current job. I began sharpening my game skills for the move. I was already good friends with the bosses who'd be opening one of the new places, so I was hired before they started officially hiring. That's how the male code works. When you're part of a team within the world of men you get the help and benefits from it. Policemen, Firemen, and players in sports leagues of all kinds know this. These social male groups are very tight-knit and hold each other's darkest secrets. That's the positive side of belonging to it. The negative side is that eventually a man will start to think and behave like his team. A man can lose himself inside it, becoming a participant in his friends immoral activities. In the social world of men we become what your friends are.

The new strip casino was becoming the talk of the town. It wouldn't be long until I'd find myself discovering much more about our code.

Chapter 7

ROYAL STATURE

Now *this is more like it*, I thought as I walked onto the casino floor for opening night. This place was incredibly opulent in every way- beautiful marble floors, huge crystal chandeliers, and a ceiling that looked like a gigantic work of art. The guests fit right in as well. This was not your typical beer drinking "average Joe" type of Crowd. The type of men who didn't just own a successful business but owned corporations, sometimes two or three. These men were your Cognac, Cuban cigar smoking men, most middle-age or older with receding hair lines. Rolex watches and golf shirts seemed to be the their everyday attire. Many arrived in Lear jets, some owned their own.

After a couple of weeks I was starting to fit right in. I made friends very quickly. I worked with many guys from my previous job as well, which was good because I could tell that some of these gamblers might become a problem. I was now a Dual-Rate Floor Supervisor, which meant sometimes I would deal games. It was a personal choice because I wanted more time with Sterling and Micheal. I also wanted to have more time to continue my writing and art projects.

I soon found out that dealing with arrogant, egotistical men was not easy. Some would fly in from their hometowns to celebrate their latest merger or big business deal. They needed a playground to spend all that money, which they did on gambling, drinking, and women… and usually in that exact order. Their wives were left sitting at home with the kids believing the promises made to them that their husband would behave himself while out in Vegas. I made friends with a couple of our big hosts so they could give me the inside on what was really going on. We dealt with high-end international players as well as the biggest celebrities and super stars on the planet. Running into nearly entire championship sports teams wasn't unusual.

Almost every night I'd hear gamblers talking about the star they'd seen the night before who'd been hanging out in the casino. The oddest thing I noticed when dealing to men with multimillion dollar casino credit lines was the special attention and rules they were given. Some of these guys could do things no regular players ever could. There's a huge difference between the fifty dollar-a-hand player and the fifty thousand dollar-a-hand player. There were some players I dealt to who would bet sixty thousand a hand on two separate hands. Men like that were treated like kings. They had their own private rooms and sometimes even tables made just for them. The problem with attention like that is that you create a monster out of the player and the dealers (usually the female ones) would be the targets of their brutal sexist behavior.

There were some millionaire players who didn't want female dealers anywhere near them. They considered them bad luck. Some didn't want female cocktail servers to approach them so they were served only by male butlers. I often would deal in the Baccarat salon and hear an angry player saying "fu**ing bitch" and other nasty things to a female dealer. These jerks knew the casino would do nothing because it was all about the money. It was unfair. These men knew the female dealer would put up with it because they needed a job for whatever reason.

There was even one situation which involved a little female dealer named Ming. We had a notoriously wicked player in the Baccarat salon one night, one of those super rich men who had been banned from a few casinos because of his bad behavior. Ming had to deal to him, unfortunately for her.

During my third break I was in the dealers break room when I heard a girl ask, "Is Ming alright?"

"I don't know," another dealer replied. Turns out that the player had lost a big bet so he grabbed a cigar ashtray and smashed Ming's hand, breaking it.

"That Mr. K is such an a**hole," I said. "It's awful how some men treat women just because they have a lot money."

From time to time I found myself in arguments with these wealthy spoiled men. Luckily my butt was always covered by my friends. I remember this one night when things got pretty bad with me and a group of three men. That night I was a Floor Supervisor and was working a section with a cocktail waitress named Victoria. I'd had my eye on her a little while. That night was going pretty smooth and I was enjoying the players and Victoria. Three guys from New York sat down wanting casino credit and drinks right away.

"Hi guys," I said, picking up their players cards. "How much you need?"

"Five thousand each," one of them said with attitude. I knew right then and there they were going to be a problem.

"Okay," I said, handing the cards to the pit clerk.

"Where's the beer bit**?" one asked loudly. I pretended not to hear him.

Seconds later I heard, "Can we get some service over here?" I walked over to the table. "She'll be right out, guys." I said, walking away to watch another table.

Not a minute later I heard, "Hey! Hey! Where's the beer bit**es around here?" he said, looking at me with a scowl.

"Give her time, you just sat down. I can't press a button and make her pop out of the table." I was starting to get angry.

"You need to give these bit***s roller-skates or something, maybe they'll move faster." I was getting tired of all his sexist remarks.

"Sir, please watch your language."

"What? We can't say 'Bi***' in a fu**ing casino?" he said in a loud voice drawing attention from players on other tables. My pit clerk immediately got on the phone sensing this was going to turn ugly.

"Take it easy," I said, trying to calm the man.

"Can't swear in a casino? This is Fu**ing Las Vegas isn't it?" his friend chimed in.

"Listen, if you keep it up, we'll have to ask you to leave."

"Fu** you, I'm not going anywhere!" he said, trying to look mad.

"No more action," I said, putting my hand over the dealer's Blackjack shoe. "Your done." I went to the podium to call my pit manager while the players continued on swearing and fussing, seconds later they crossed the line.

"Fu** you!" one said from behind me. "I'll have you fired!"

"NO, FU** YOU!" I said, losing my temper. Just as my pit boss walked over.

"WHOA! WHOA! WHOA! What's going on, Josh?"

I briefly explained to Tom what had happened. He sent me on break telling me he'd handle it. After my break I went back up and the guys were gone. Tom pulled me aside.

"Still have that temper, huh?" he said, smiling.

"Tom, those cocky pieces of sh** pushed me too far."

"I'll take care of it, Josh," he said, patting my back. "Relax."

"Thanks Tom. I owe you one." I knew Tom from my old job. Thank God he was there to save my butt. Anyone else would have been fired on the spot for swearing at a guest. This was one of those times when being part of the code really helped.

It felt good defending the waitress. Who would have imagined me stepping up to defend a woman I barely knew just because it seemed right? To be honest, I'd do it again and again because it was such a good feeling…

⁂ ⁂ ⁂ ⁂ ⁂

I was constantly scheduled in the high stakes private rooms. Management liked to put me there because I rarely lost. As a dealer I was incredibly hard to beat. I gained this reputation by beating a problem player out of more than a million dollars in less than thirty minutes. I was nicknamed "Million" by some of the bosses because of it. I could be supervising in a section and get a call to put on a dealer's uniform to replace a dealer who would be losing to a million dollar player. I'd be told, "Do your thing, Million." I rarely let them down. Everyone loves a winner.

I also began to master an Chinese game called Pai gow Tiles. It was a game I'd been dealing for a few years. It was rare to have an American know it to near master levels. People who play this game are very judgmental. There can be extreme prejudice towards anyone not Asian who deals it. I proved that you didn't have to be Asian to deal it. The game was intimidating to most because of the fifty thousand to sixty thousand dollar-a-hand players. I earned my respect. I was even told that I deal better than most people they'd ever seen. I'd even gotten offers to deal it in Macau and California for private gambling parties.

I met a lot of very interesting people when dealing and supervising that game, many singers and actors from Asia, as well as many big business men from China and Taiwan. I even dealt to Asian royalty at times. I started to build relationships with some of these big players. Mr. Lau was one of them. Mr. Lau was a Taiwanese software giant. He and his companions, Danny and Sam loved the game and my company. They would fly in once every couple of months and request me to deal to them. I didn't mind. Mr. Lau was a big tipper and always in a good mood. He spoke very little English so Danny and Sam would help interpret for him.

Mr. Lau was the type of guy who would lose a quarter million dollars and still have a smile on his face. He seemed to really enjoy life, even when he lost. I liked that about him. I was often asked to hang out with them after work. I usually declined, but on one particular night I decided to take them up on their offer.

We meet at another casino just down the Las Vegas Strip. I took an early out and went home to change. I gave Danny a call from my cell phone to let him know I was on my way.

"We will be in the High Limit area," Danny said.

"Okay, will I be able to bet quarters?" I asked.

"Don't worry about money, we take care of you," Danny replied with his heavy Mandarin accent. About an hour later I was walking towards their table. Mr. Lau had stacks of thousands and hundreds in front of him.

"Hey brotha," Danny said, stepping away from the table to greet me. I hugged Danny and bowed to Mr. Lau.

"Sit. Sit," Mr. Lau said, smiling. Danny pulled out a chair for me. "You guys doing okay?" I asked.

"Eh, So, so." Danny said. "What you drinking tonight?"

"I'm feeling like a Kamikaze."

Danny looked at the waitress standing near the table. "Kamikaze for my friend."

I noticed that one of the chairs next to the table had two purses sitting on it.

"Who's purses?" I asked, looking at Danny and Mr. Lau, who smiled and nodded a little.

"Our friends," Danny replied. Mr. Lau threw two yellow chips in front of me.

"Play," he said, motioning with his hand. I paused for a minute.

"Two thousand?" I said, looking at Mr. Lau.

"For you," he replied.

"That's yours, brotha," Danny said. I pretended it was too much by shaking my head.

"Thank you," I said, nodding after a few seconds. I changed it down to five hundred-dollar chips. The dealer was kind of quiet, probably wondering why I was out with a huge multi-million dollar player.

"Nine teen-bo," I said, looking at my hand.

"Nice hand," Danny said. "Going to be a lucky night for you."

"I hope so."

"We're back," I heard someone say from behind me. I turned to see two very thin Asian ladies in cocktail dresses.

"This is Joshua," Danny said, introducing me.

"Hi," I said, shaking their hands and nodding. They took their seats to the right of me.

Danny put his right arm around me and spoke in my ear. "Which one do you want?"

"I looked at him with raised eyebrow, then smiled. "Oh," I said, now looking over at Mr. Lau.

"Mr. Lau got them for us," Danny whispered.

I was a little shocked. I smiled at Mr. Lau and nodded as if to say 'thank you.' I turned to see the two girls looking at me, talking to each other in mandarin and smiling. *Oh boy*, I thought, this could be trouble. I decided to just keep gambling until I figured out what I wanted to do. This was a first, being offered women as a gift. *This isn't going to be easy for me at all*, I thought. They were both very attractive, so I tried to make as little eye contact with them as possible.

As the night went on and I was now on my second kamikaze, one moved her chair closer to mine. It was leather cushion to leather cushion. I guess she had made the choice for me. Soon I felt her hand on my knee. With every hand we played, her hand seemed to move higher and higher up my thigh.

"Excuse me," I said, leaving the table and heading for the men's room. I decided to go there to figure things out.

I returned minutes later with my lie about a problem at home with the babysitter.

"Mr. Lau, Danny I'm sorry I have to cut this short, but I need to get home."

"Aww," Danny said, looking a little disappointed.

"Please tell Mr. Lau I apologize."

I tried to hand the chips back to Mr. Lau, but he pushed it back in my hand.

"Yours," he said, smiling and nodding.

"Thank you," I said, nodding. I shook their hands and made haste to the casino cage to cash out. I ended up making an extra fifteen hundred from the two thousand I already had. Danny was right, it was a lucky night for me after all. *The life of a millionaire,* I thought as I walked to the valet. *Must be a blast.*

I had always been told by my friends in the casino host department what the very wealthy do, but to actually get a taste of it was awesome. It's no wonder wealthy men have mistresses. How could they not? I remember the Saudi royals who would come in from time to time. We always knew when they were in town because of the fleet of black trucks parked all around the hotel. I wondered what it would be like to be worth billions and have all the women you wanted. *It couldn't possibly get boring,* I decided. I guess that's why they have multiple wives to keep them out of trouble and very, very busy.

$$\bullet \ \bullet \ \bullet \ \bullet \ \bullet$$

I've found that men who are worth millions of dollars are also tremendously sexist. I think it's because they have women throwing themselves at them constantly. A good example of this happened the night I had one of the biggest names in pro basketball sit down to play on one of my tables. He and other professional players were in town for a basketball clinic. These were times when players and coaches would come out and let men try out for possible spots on professional teams. Nights like this also brought out all the very pretty, money-driven women looking to bag a millionaire.

This player sat down along with two of his teammates and a couple of friends. He also had his agent and an assistant nearby. Many of these guys travel with an entourage. He had only just begun to play when he started to draw attention from male fans waving and yelling his name and, of course, the young ladies walking around the casino looking for the big money players. He wasn't dressed up; in fact he was dressed down in common street clothes, jeans, tennis shoes, and a very average green shirt which had a team logo on it. He had on big sunglasses and no jewelry at all. That didn't stop the female attention though.

"Excuse me," said a young lady wearing a salmon-colored, tight-fitting party dress. "I was wondering if I could get a picture with you?" She was very polite. Three of her friends were standing back watching.

"No, I don't do pictures," he said arrogantly. One of her friends in a black cat-suit walked a little closer and started to sort of dance for all the men standing around him, thrusting her pelvis back and fourth in a sexual way to the casino music. Another was playing with her breasts, acting like she was adjusting them, mostly just trying to draw attention to them. It was like watching a live audition and it was all for "him," Mr. Star Athlete.

"Sorry to disturb you. Have a good night," said the first girl away. The star player watched her walk away. "I wouldn't mind smashing that now that I see that big a**," he said.

"Yeah, we could put her in the truck and make her take care of us all for your autograph," one of his friends said, laughing.

I felt sorry for that young woman and her friends. They were doing nothing but surrendering themselves to men who just wanted to disrespect them in the worst kind of ways. *Where was their dignity?*

I wondered. Is money really that important to women? If these young ladies could just focus, get an education, they could be as successful as him. To me there's no reason to submit to anybody, especially not to a man who will degrade you.

I continued to meet more and more exceptional people. One of my favorite players was a Sikh from India who I called "the Guru." Guru was an older man in his early sixties who would often visit with his wife and her brother. He was a nice change from the usual pompous, uppity, sexist, corporate phony men. We had real conversations about politics, religion, and philosophy. On one of his trips he brought a friend of his I called "Julian." The reason for the nickname was because to me he looked like a suave guy who should be named Julian. He was about forty years old, well-dressed, and very animated. This guy had an incredible amount of energy and charisma. Very soon I'd see Julian use his charm to do something I'd never seen a man do before.

It was a big weekend in Vegas. The casino was hosting a Baccarat tournament and a huge concert. It was also the weekend that the Magic convention was in town. Magic was a huge clothing convention which took place once a year in Vegas. It brings out the biggest names in the fashion business. It also brings those who have large underworld ties. I was working just outside the high limit salon so I'd get some of these people on my games. One of these more dangerous types was playing in my pit on one of the tables.

Word around town was that this particular man ran a high end international prostitution ring. I'd been watching him whenever he stayed at the hotel and noticed that when he wasn't with his gang of Russian-speaking friends, he'd be with three to five very quiet, beautiful women. Two of them had matching tattoos on their necks which I found out from certain sources was a kind of label of his product. I also noticed he was trying to get closer and closer to some of the cocktail waitresses. I guess he was always looking for more girls to add to his business. He'd be very charming to them and tip them one hundred dollars per drink.

The more experienced girls would thank him and keep moving because they were in the know, but there was one that wasn't so experienced, a very young girl from Seattle I called "Mal" short for "Malibu." She was one of those extremely pretty girls: long blonde hair, dark eye brows, blue eyes, and slightly tanned skin. She had a certain innocence about her and reminded me of a living Malibu Barbie doll. Most, if not all of the other waitresses were jealous of her naturally good looks. The Russian guy definitely had an eye on her.

"Hey Guru," I said, coming back from break to see him sitting at a Blackjack table.

"Joshua! Wonderful to see you again, my friend," he said, in his smooth bollywood, Indian accent. "I have someone for you to meet." I was introduced to Julian.

"It's a pleasure to meet you," he said.

"You too, Sir," I replied. I shuffled the cards and started the game.

"Wasn't that Herman Cain, the guy from T.V. I saw you talking too earlier?" Guru asked.

"Yeah, H.C. He likes three-card poker. I've played with him a few times now. We get a lot of big shots strolling through, everyone from Rupert Murdock to Will I Am."

"I bet you see it all." Julian said sitting down.

"Over the years I've learned all kinds of things about a lot of famous people."

"Met any really big stars?"

"Sure, Shaq, Jordan, Gretzky, the list goes on. From time to time I do private hosting so I get to mingle with a lot of big shots. Mostly the wealthy business types."

"Any famous women?"

"Rhianna was playing right where your sitting about a month ago."

"Wow! I'd love to met her, she is so beautiful."

"Yeah, she's got some serious sex-appeal, she's much sexier in person.

"There are so many women here. Is this common?" asked Julian.

"For a weekend like this, yes. There's a lot going on," I replied. "Concert, conventions, and tournament."

"I see," Julian said. "You must love it here. You get paid to look at women all night long."

"Well, I do love the sights, but it's still work." Minutes later I heard, "Cocktails, drinks anyone?"

"Please, please," Guru said, stopping Mal.

"Oh my, what a beautiful flower," Julian said, staring at Mal.

"Thank you," she said in a soft tone.

"Johnny Walker black, please," said Julian.

"I'd like tea. Thank you," said Guru.

"Okay," Mal said cheerfully. "I'll be right back"

"Wow!" said Julian with a big smile. "She is special."

As I chatted and dealt to Julian and Guru I noticed Mal talking to the Russian and his friend in front of the High-Limit salon from time to time as she made her drink passes. There was no question he was spinning his web.

Later I took a thirty-minute break. Upon my return, I asked, "How's it going?" I saw that Guru had ditched his tea for a Johnny Walker.

"Very good," Julian said. I could tell he was starting to feel the effects of his drink. There was a table next to their's where three guys and a young lady were sitting. The three guys were playing and the lady was just watching. You see this many times in casinos. I always wonder why women will just sit there watching the men have a good time. I guess Julian didn't like it either.

"EXCUSE ME! EXCUSE ME!" he yelled towards the next table. The lady at the table turned towards him. "Come here," he said, waving his hand. "I want to speak with you, please." To my amazement, she came and stood next to him. "Have a seat, please," he told her. I couldn't wait to see where this was headed. "Are you having a good time?" Julian asked.

"Yes," the lady said softly.

"You don't look like you are. I want you to have fun."

"Okay, she said, smiling a little.

"Who are those guys with you, your friends?"

"One is my husband. The other two are his friends." I couldn't believe my ears.

"How long have you been married?" Julian asked.

"About a year and a half."

"You're a beautiful young woman. You deserve to be happy." Julian went on and on charming her for the next thirty minutes.

I was sent on another break, returning a short time later. "Where's your new girlfriend?" I asked because it was just Guru and Julian now playing.

"I made her feel good and sent her on her way."

"Julian, I can't believe she was married and sat down with you. That takes huge balls."

"This woman is very unhappy. You see, she is not in a marriage of love. She is in a marriage of convenience. She will probably never get love so I try to give her what I can because I love all women," Julian said, standing away from the table opening his arms wide like he was giving the world a hug. I just smiled at him. I found out later that Julian had called the husband over while I was on break and had given him some words of wisdom regarding a woman's needs. That night I realized I wasn't the only man who loved and enjoyed women so much.

A little later on that night I saw Mal speaking with the Russian man again. He was holding her arm as they spoke, working his way into her life. I decided it was time to let her know what she was about to get herself into, so on her next pass around the tables I stopped her.

"Mal!" I said, motioning with my hand for her to come closer.

"Hi Josh," she said in her sweet bubbly voice. "What's up?"

"Because you are a very attractive young lady, you need to be very careful. You know the guy over there that you were talking to earlier?" I said, pointing to the area where the Russian had been holding her arm. "Word is he's involved in some pretty dangerous activities."

"Like what?" she asked with interest.

"Well, let's just say there is a very good chance he's involved in high-end prostitution."

A look of fright swept across her face. "You're serious?"

"Very, so just be careful with him, okay?"

"Oh my God! Tonight he asked me if I could join him in los Angeles next weekend." I just remained silent letting her digest the news. "Wow!" she said seconds later.

"Thank you, Josh."

"It's my pleasure, doll. I just don't want to see you get caught up in something you aren't prepared to deal with. Just be careful. The world is full of deception, babe."

"Thank you so much," she said, leaving the table.

I felt really good about possibly preventing a horrible mistake. I wonder what would have happened if I'd never said anything and let her fall into his hands that night. If only more men would step in to prevent dangers to women instead of ignoring them our society would be so much better off.

• • • • •

One warm July seventh morning while driving to work I had strangest feeling that something big was coming. Little did I know that this was the day I would be introduced to a lady who would change the direction of my life forever. Her name was K.O. She was a slender Vietnamese woman in her late twenties with long black hair and a big beautiful smile that complimented her amazing personality. That night when we met neither she nor I wanted to stop shaking each other's hand. I knew this was going to be serious trouble. After our first break we ended up walking side by side to the employee dining room to get coffee.

"You like chess?" she asked.

"Sure." Chess was a big thing on our breaks. I'd been playing for some time and wasn't easy to beat. I knew a few strategies that I'd had some very good success with.

"Let's play." I led her to one of the many chess tables we'd set up.

"Take it easy on me," I said, sitting down. She picked white and moved first.

"What's the wager?" I asked, really looking at her up close for the first time.

"Humm." she said, looking in my eyes. "I want what whatever you want." I could see she wanted to play more than just a game of chess.

"Loser takes the winner out wherever they want," she said, smiling and staring. Her eyes seemed to smile when she stared at me.

"You're on." I soon realized this girl could really play. "How did you get so good at this game?"

She went on to tell me how she had been playing since she was a little girl and how she was a *straight-A* student in school. I was getting my butt kicked by her.

"You're in big trouble," she said, smiling. Minutes later she'd trapped my queen. "Bye, Bye queen," she whispered.

"Oh my god! No fair, you're distracting me," I said.

"How?"

"Your shirt is sort of open." It really wasn't. I was making up cute excuses just to do it. She laughed. I was soon check-mated. "Guess I'm paying," I said cheerfully. "You're good."

She was so happy that she'd beaten me. You could see it all over her face. This wasn't the first time I'd been beaten by a woman. Micheal and I had many good chess matches at home. I'd usually win, but Micheal did kick my butt sometimes.

It was time to go back to the casino floor. "See you next break," she said, walking off to her table.

After a couple of days K.O. and I grew closer and closer. We didn't always see each other because of our breaks, but when we did, all we did was talk. I found out that she worked another dealing job and had two children who lived out of state, which I thought was a little strange. How could a mother stand to be away from her small children? I remember asking if she had a boyfriend. She looked sort of nervous and said, "Not anymore."

"What happened?" I asked. "Because you're a great girl."

"He wasn't so great," she replied, losing her smile.

"I hope he wasn't abusive."

"That and much more. I don't want to talk about him."

"Sorry," I said. I could tell she'd been through something terrible. I hate abusive men more than anything.

"Do you have a girlfriend?" she asked.

"No, babe, I'm married." She was a little surprised.

"You don't look married."

"What does married look like?" I said, chuckling. "Over-weight, boring, and defeated?" I asked.

"Right, that's a start," she said. I showed her pictures of my daughter and of Micheal.

"Your wife is beautiful," she said, obviously a little intimidated by the picture.

"Thank you, that's my girl."

She showed me pictures of her two daughters. They were about two and three years old in the picture. "They are so cute," I said, smiling.

"Thank you. I hope to get them back." I thought maybe she'd somehow lost custody of them or something. There was more going on than I knew, but that just drew me closer to her.

"When you taking me out? You owe me," she asked.

"Maybe this weekend. I have to clear it with Micheal first."

"What? You're gonna tell her?" She got a little nervous.

"Yeah. She and I have an honest relationship. Don't worry, I've been out before with other women." K.O. was shocked that I was so honest. I guess she had never met a man who was.

"I really don't want to start any trouble," she said.

"Don't worry, if there's trouble I will deal with it, not you. We exchanged numbers that day in the break room.

One morning after dropping my daughter off to school, I pulled into the garage and saw Micheal smoking a cigarette, obviously waiting for me.

"Hey, baby," I said, closing the car door.

"What's going on?" she asked, looking at me with a funny expression.

"Huh?" I replied.

"Last couple of days you've been different." Somehow she knew I had a little crush on someone. It's amazing how women can tell.

"Well, to be honest I met someone at work who's pretty cool. I was actually going to tell you about it today but you beat me to it."

"What's her name?"

"K.O. She just started, I said, nodding. I was planning on taking her out for a bite to eat"

"What's she look like?"

"She's okay I guess, kinda cute." She could tell she was more than cute. Micheal looked at me like she was trying to read me.

"You really like this girl," she said with a serious look. I decided to be more honest.

"Well," I said, taking a seat next to her in the garage. I must admit I do like her. There's something strange about her."

"She's trouble then," Micheal said.

"I don't know, babe."

"When are you two going out?"

"I was thinking this weekend if you don't mind."

"I don't own you, Josh. Do your thing. Be careful with this one." Micheal could sense something. I always liked that about her. I also respected her for trusting me to do the right thing.

A few days later K.O. and I met at a restaurant and bar before work. She had on her work uniform and tennis shoes. We sat down in a booth and placed our orders. We talked about work when we weren't flirting with each other. When our food arrived she immediately started cutting it for me. "You don't have to do that, babe, I got it."

"I want to," she said with a smile. While eating her food, she kept looking at me over and over.

"Something wrong?" I asked.

"Nope," she said, continuing to take peeks at me. I didn't know what she was thinking. It was very strange. Maybe she had a crush too. We chatted for an hour or so, then went to look at the night sky. It was a very nice date. Neither of us really came on to the other, we just sort of hung out as friends, even though there was some serious chemistry there. It felt like we'd known each other for years. As the days went on K.O. and I started flirting a little more seriously, a lot of hand touching when we talked, along with hugs and cheek kisses when we'd go home.

K.O. liked to be alone with me on the elevator. There were times when people would try to get on and she'd tell them, "Sorry, full, get the next one." She could be very brash when she wanted to be. If we were sitting together in the break room she would tell whoever sat near us to sit somewhere else. If I was walking into work I would hear her calling my name and rushing to walk with me. This was getting serious. She wanted to go out again with me. I decided I needed to talk to Micheal about this situation because I was becoming very confused. Micheal was already feeling my change and she wasn't happy about it. I summoned up the courage to ask her to meet with me and K.O. for lunch. Micheal wanted to meet the girl given how smitten I appeared to be.

We all drove to the same bar where K.O. and I had drinks and appetizers a couple of weeks prior. After the waitress took our orders, I started the conversation.

"Well," I said, smiling, "we look good." We all smiled at each other.

"So you're K.O.," Micheal said, looking across the table. I made sure to sit between them in the booth. "You're much better looking than Josh had described.

"Thank you," K.O. said, smiling. They were both so very calm, like we were all family.

"I understand you like Josh a lot?" K.O. smiled and nodded, taking a sip from her cocktail. "He's a good man. You have good taste." Micheal said, now looking at me.

"I really, really like him," K.O. admitted. "There's something about him, I can't really explain." I just sat there looking at the two of them thinking, *This is awesome. Here I am with two beautiful women discussing me.*

The ladies continued to get to know each other while I was figuring out what the hell my next move would be. I decided to throw something out to see what their reaction would be. "Ladies, is there any way we could all be in a relationship?"

"You would love that I'm sure," Micheal said, looking hard at me.

"What do you think K.O.?" I asked.

"I'd have to think about it," she replied.

"I mean we all seem to get along, so why not?" I figured we all had to be thinking about it anyway. Of course it was every man's dream to have two great women. Most would think I was trying to have it all, but in all honesty I really liked them both. Micheal was my wife and I still felt a lot of love for her and didn't want to lose her, but I also had strong feelings for K.O. I wrapped up the lunch with a kiss and hug from both of my girls and drove home.

At home, Micheal spoke her mind. "She seems to be into you, Josh, but I won't share you. I'm not anyone's fool." She was pissed.

"It was just a suggestion, babe, that's all. I'm a little screwed up with the whole thing myself."

I knew I had crossed the line.

"Do you love me anymore?" she asked.

"Yes, babe, I love you. I also want to be honest with you. I like this girl a lot."

"Do you love her?" She asked, growing more and more angry.

"I don't think so, I don't know what I feel." The argument went on and on into the night. From that night on our relationship was different. *So much for total honesty,* I thought. Maybe it was better to just run off and cheat like most men do.

After a few days of soul searching I decided to distance myself from K.O. I had too much at stake. I had money, a new, semi-custom home, and a good family. I sat with K.O. at work one night and told her we needed to slow things down a bit. She listened, but the following day when I saw her she was visibly different. Her hair was not done and her clothes weren't ironed. Her make-up was barely there as well. I knew I had broken yet another heart. I felt horrible.

Weeks had passed and I still had feelings for K.O. She and I shared passing glances, but that was about it. I noticed her talking to some of the older bosses, almost charming them. One day she came in with a cast on her thumb. I thought, *Who the hell gets a broken thumb? so* I decided to ask her about it.

"Hey, babe, come here a minute, please." It was early morning and we were in the break room. She slowly walked over and sat down next to me. We locked eyes and that old chemistry started bubbling back up between us. "What happened to your thumb?"

"Oh, it's nothing. I fell rollerblading."

"You never told me you rollerbladed," I said, giving her a puzzled look.

"I have to go." She stood up and went to the ladies room. I wondered what the hell was wrong with her. I sat back and observed her in the weeks following. I later heard about her offering rides home to older managers and supervisors we worked with which was very strange because these guys didn't need rides home. I decided to give her a call and feel her out.

"Hey, babe, it's Josh. What's going on?"

"Nothing, just finished getting a new Tattoo."

"Oh yeah, what did you get?" I asked.

"Sin on the back of my neck."

"The word 'sin'?" I asked.

"Yep."

"Interesting." I said, knowing that usually prostitutes get tattoos like that. I thought, *nah, she can't be hooking, she works two jobs.* "Hey, you've been on my mind lately. You miss me?"

"Josh," she started, then paused. "I like you too much, I have to go." She hung up the phone. *What in the hell does that mean?* I wondered. This was getting more weird by the day. I decided I needed to clear my head, so we went on a vacation.

Micheal, Sterling, and I drove to Laguna California to spend a week on the beach. We loved the beach there and it was a good time for our yearly family get away.

Micheal needed a good vacation. She was still angry with me, so I was hoping it would smooth things out.

• • • • •

Upon returning from Laguna, Micheal and I sat down to discuss our relationship. She informed me that she'd be looking for a place of her own and that I'd soon be served with divorce papers. I didn't argue her decision. I know nothing in life last forever. I was crushed, but always the warrior, I didn't let it show.

I returned to work. While looking up my schedule for the week I noticed K.O.'s name wasn't listed. I thought it was odd, so later I visited the scheduling office to speak with Dominic, the casino scheduling manager.

"Hey, Dom," I said, walking into his office.

"Josh! How was Laguna?"

"It was okay. Hey, what's up with K.O.? She's not on the schedule." Everyone knew K.O. and I had something going on.

"I'm not suppose to talk about this, but your girl got fired for soliciting." I was dumbfounded. How could I have been so blind? Suddenly the puzzle pieces started to fit. Her abusive boyfriend, no doubt a pimp. Her broken thumb, no doubt done by his hand. The playful sexual advances on wealthy players and bosses. The kids living out of state, bargaining chips to keep her working and under control. I wondered how such a smart, well-spoken, beautiful woman could fall into such a bad situation. Living in constant fear for her children and herself, seen as nothing more than a reusable product to some man probably disguised as a respectable credit counselor somewhere. I had seen this time and time again when hanging around rich, and powerful men, but I never thought I would be directly involved.

Chapter 8

A SHOCKING TRUTH

For the next couple of days I wasn't myself and management was starting to notice. I felt so stupid. I kept beating myself up about the whole thing. I couldn't believe I had been so blind. For one thing I had completely ruined my marriage with Micheal. I knew I had made one of the biggest mistakes of my life and it wasn't easy to deal with. I was also angry with K.O. for not just telling me the truth. If she'd just told me what was going on, maybe I could have helped her out somehow.

I was supervising a casino pit just outside of the High Limit area when I got a phone call from Walter, the Director of Casino Operations.

"Joshua, I'm sending down Monica to take your section for a little while, I need to speak with you."

"Okay, is something wrong?" I asked.

"No, I just need to speak with you."

"Ok, Sir" I hung up the phone feeling a little confused. I wondered what was going on. I was sure I hadn't done anything wrong.

I knew only little about Walter. he was about fifty five years old, very serious, and was one of those guys who was very connected in all sorts of ways. His title was "Director of Casino Operations," but the rumor was that he was much more than that. He took a liking to me early on and had mentioned to me a couple of times that he wanted to see me go far in the business. He was one of those guys who was making a six-figure salary and receiving massive bonuses on top of that each and every year.

Five minutes later Monica arrived and I headed to Casino Operations offices. I entered and waited outside of Walter's office until his secretary said it was okay to enter.

"Joshua, have a seat," Walter said without taking his eyes off of the surveillance screens. "Mosh, will be joining us, I hope you don't mind?"

"Not at all," I replied trying to sound nonchalant even though I was starting to feel a little nervous.

Mosh was a complete mystery to most. He was a gentleman who people in management both feared and respected. He called himself a "host," but no one ever saw him really do any work at all. He usually appeared when we had the owner of the casino on property or when we had foreign dignitaries as guests.

Mosh was a charming man, about sixty three years old, who had worked in the casino business for more than thirty years. I once had a conversation with him and I remember him saying he'd spent time in South Africa opening casinos long ago. He was an international figure, with family members who were investment bankers. He was often traveling to Macau, China on business and spoke with a unique accent.

Having both of these guys speak with me at the same time was very unusual. I was either in some serious trouble or I was about to be given a very special assignment. I stood up as Mosh entered the room. "Hello Sir," I said, shaking his hand.

"Ah, Joshua. How are you feeling young man?" he said, smiling.

"Pretty good."

"Wonderful," Mosh said, taking a seat next to mine in front of Walters desk.

Walter wasted no time getting to the point. "Joshua. I called you here because I understand you had a relationship with Ms. K.O."

"Well, I wouldn't call it a relationship, sir. We went out a couple of times that was about it."

"I'm sure you know what happened." Walter said.

"When I got back from vacation I was told she was fired for soliciting. That's about all I know. To be honest, Sir, I was blown away when I heard that. I had no idea she was a prostitute." I decided to be totally honest with Walter. I had nothing to hide anyway.

"She never propositioned you?" Walter asked.

"Nope, It was the strangest thing. Now that I know, I've been wondering why she didn't."

Probably because she really liked you. You're a handsome young man." Mosh said, jumping into the conversation.

"Thank you, Sir. I don't know what she was thinking, but I'm a little broken up by the whole thing to be honest."

"How so?" Walter asked.

"Before I tell you, could we agree that everything I tell you never leaves this room? It's pretty embarrassing to me."

"Of course." Mosh said.

"We agree." Walter said.

"Well, first off-my wife knew everything." I shifted nervously in my chair.

"Everything?" Walter asked.

"Everything."

"Why the hell did you do that? Walter said.

"You are kidding?" Mosh asked.

"I wish I was." I said, glancing at Mosh. "My wife and I made an agreement when we got married to always tell the truth to each other, no matter what. I'm a man who lives up to his promises."

"Wow! I knew I liked you, Josh. Very few men would have been so honest." Walter said, shaking his head a little.

"I believe that honesty is everything. If every man would just be honest with the woman in their life, I think we would all win. No lies, no deception, just be honest."

"What did that honesty get you?" Walter asked.

"I'm sure you already know." I said, looking at Walter. "A divorce, but I can sleep at night knowing I was completely honest. How many men can do that?"

"Not any I know," Walter said, looking at Mosh. Mosh Chuckled a little.

"No one I know either," Mosh said.

"I had no clue that prostitution ran so deep. Who would have thought that a woman would be working as a high-end prostitute and working Forty hours at a great job at the same time? This just blew my mind."

"It's seems you were inadvertently pulled into something few people ever get to see, Joshua. There's much more going on in the world than most will ever know." Walter said, looking directly into my eyes. I knew then that both of these men had serious secrets.

"Women like your friend K.O. aren't as rare as you may think. The part-time prostitute is everywhere and in every profession, It is and always will be the biggest business in the world. She was probably raised to be a prostitute, sold into prostitution at an early age, and trained to become a professional. We're seeing more and more of this"

"You mean by her family?" I asked.

"Yes, of course. It's hard for Americans to understand because we haven't lived in a third world country. Her father probably sold her."

"Wow!" I said, shaking my head. "How could a father do that."

"It's happening more and more, Joshua," Mosh said. "Unfortunately it's the way of the world. There are professional prostitutes out there with master's degrees. You've been in this business for a while now, you know what's really going on. How many married men do you see every week going up to their suites with beautiful young call girls? I'm willing to bet that there isn't a single suite in Las Vegas which hasn't had an escort working in it. We all love beautiful women. Most of those girls were lured into it prostitution through phony modeling companies. Human trafficking and sex slavery is a huge business all over the world, especially in Asian countries like Cambodia, Laos and China. Those people will do anything they can in order to have a life in America. I've seen little girls prostituted in these countries with my own eyes, Josh. Children."

"Women in America aren't exactly free either, you know." Walter said. "They are the biggest slaves to big business. Mechanic's, electricians, plumbers and others make billion's from women by service stacking them. A good example is in car repair. Women immediately take their car in for service when that engine light comes on, right?"

"Right." I said, listening closely.

"You and I know its just bullshit half the time, usually a gas cap not tight or a burned out sensor, but to a woman who knows nothing about cars she's an easy target. She'll get taken for hundred's of dollars or more. They lead in with the complimentary inspection which will always point out problems she doesn't have in order to charge her for things she doesn't need when actually all she needed to do was to tighten her gas cap. Women have always been victimized by men, because they can't see the real world. Just be happy you were born a man."

I sat there listening to Walter and thinking to myself, this has got to change. *There needs to be a wake-up call.* Here I was talking with two very worldly, educated, and well-informed men and learning that the code of men was indeed a global one.

"To be honest Joshua, I think K.O. cared for you," Mosh said. "She just wasn't able to tell you the truth. You see, some believe that in many third world countries their own governments may be behind it. She probably was working to build a client list and at the same time being led to believe she could have a career after working off her debt to her owner, which of course a complete lie. These men have made millions off of these girls, why would they let them go? The truth is, they own them for life."

"Do yourself a favor, Joshua. Forget about K.O. and move on. You're a sharp young man. Make lots of money and enjoy the world." Walter said.

"This young man deserves a break." Mosh said, smiling at me.

"Joshua, I'd like you to take two weeks off. I think you could use a break with this K.O. situation and the divorce," Walter said.

"That's a good idea, Sir, Thank you."

"I'll have your paper work ready by the end of the day. Go see Dominic in scheduling tomorrow."

"Thank you." I said standing up. "Well this has certainly been an eye opener to say the least," I said, smiling and shaking hands, first Walter's and then Mosh's. I walked out of the meeting feeling a bit dispirited. I had learned what I had always suspected-that men of high position and power know all too well what's happening in the world around them, but do nothing to help. Like most wealthy men, they would rather take whatever they can from the world and ignore its Problems, turning their backs on the women of the world who need all the help they can get. I decided I wouldn't just take it easy and forget about what was really going on and what I knew. It was time to write the wake-up call.

· · · · ·

While driving home after work that evening, I began to ponder the idea of a world with complete gender balance in positions of leadership and what it would mean to America and the women of the world. I began to smile as I could see myself turning on the television in the near future and seeing an American Congress with a dominant female presence. For so long the truth had been secretly kept just out of their reach. Now women would finally know the truth, finally know the secrets of our male code. Women would finally have the most guarded information to create positive changes which would influence great female leaders of today, tomorrow, and beyond. That time is now.

For more information about Mark Million visit:

MarkMillion.net

Twitter.com/AuthorMMillion

Facebook.com/AuthorMarkMillion

BUY A SHARE OF THE FUTURE IN YOUR COMMUNITY

These certificates make great holiday, graduation and birthday gifts that can be personalized with the recipient's name. The cost of one S.H.A.R.E. or one square foot is $54.17. The personalized certificate is suitable for framing and will state the number of shares purchased and the amount of each share, as well as the recipient's name. The home that you participate in "building" will last for many years and will continue to grow in value.

Here is a sample SHARE certificate:

THIS CERTIFIES THAT

YOUR NAME HERE

HAS INVESTED IN A HOME FOR A DESERVING FAMILY

1985-2010

TWENTY-FIVE YEARS OF BUILDING FUTURES
IN OUR COMMUNITY ONE HOME AT A TIME

1200 SQUARE FOOT HOUSE @ $65,000 = $54.17 PER SQUARE FOOT
This certificate represents a tax deductible donation. It has no cash value.

YES, I WOULD LIKE TO HELP!

I support the work that Habitat for Humanity does and I want to be part of the excitement! As a donor, I will receive periodic updates on your construction activities but, more importantly, I know my gift will help a family in our community realize the dream of homeownership. **I would like to SHARE in your efforts against substandard housing in my community!** *(Please print below)*

PLEASE SEND ME _____ SHARES at $54.17 EACH = $ $_____

In Honor Of: _____

Occasion: (Circle One)   HOLIDAY   BIRTHDAY   ANNIVERSARY

OTHER: _____

Address of Recipient: _____

Gift From: _____ *Donor Address:* _____

Donor Email: _____

I AM ENCLOSING A CHECK FOR $ $_____ PAYABLE TO HABITAT FOR HUMANITY **OR** PLEASE CHARGE MY VISA OR MASTERCARD *(CIRCLE ONE)*

Card Number _____ Expiration Date: _____

Name as it appears on Credit Card _____ Charge Amount $ _____

Signature _____

Billing Address _____

Telephone # Day _____ Eve _____

PLEASE NOTE: Your contribution is tax-deductible to the fullest extent allowed by law.
Habitat for Humanity • P.O. Box 1443 • Newport News, VA 23601 • 757-596-5553
www.HelpHabitatforHumanity.org

Printed in the USA
CPSIA information can be obtained
at www.ICGtesting.com
JSHW022345140824
68134JS00019B/1692